Getting the Most out of Your U.S. History Course

The History Student's Vade Mecum

Neil R. Stout
University of Vermont

D. C. Heath and Company
Lexington, Massachusetts   Toronto

Published simultaneously in Canada.

Printed in the United States of America.

International Standard Book Number: 0-669-33239-9

0 9 8 7 6 5 4 3 2 1

Preface

In 1950 I started college. I was an Ohio farm boy who had never been west of Chicago or east of Pittsburgh, though I had read a lot of history, enjoyed it, and thought I understood it. I traveled from Parkersburg, West Virginia, to Cambridge, Massachusetts, by train (neither jet airplanes nor interstate highways were available yet). When classes started, as you can well imagine, I didn't have a clue about how to study, take exams, write papers, or much of anything else. I survived, but it was a pretty close call. I've spent the intervening forty years learning how to do these things.

I have also learned that while students today are a lot more sophisticated than I was, they don't know a great deal more than I did about how to survive a history course. Some years ago, I started handing out a mimeographed guide that I called *The History Student's Vade Mecum* to help my students at the University of Vermont get through my survey course in American history. They received it well, and many of them made suggestions for improvements, additions, deletions, and so on. So did my graduate teaching assistants. This guide, then, is the product of not just my own experience but also that of several thousand students. A few years ago, I gave a copy to a sales representative from D. C. Heath and Company. She suggested that it might be worthy of a wider audience — namely you. Here it is. I believe it will help.

Neil R. Stout

Acknowledgments

Author and publisher gratefully acknowledge the fine suggestion made by the following historians in the course of the developmen of this guide:

Harriet E. Amos, University of Alabama, Birmingham
Wendy F. Hamand, Eastern Illinois University
Joseph M. Hawes, Memphis State University
Joe Jaynes, Collin County Community College District
Michael L. Kurtz, Southeastern Louisiana University
Harmon Mothershead, Northwest Missouri State University
Douglas W. Richmond, University of Texas, Arlington

Contents

Contents

1. Studying History

What makes a college course in U.S. history different from the one I had in high school?

The students

You and your fellow students make the most striking difference. You have decided to come to college, to join an intellectual community, in order to further your education. In general, colleges and universities expect students to do far more reading, writing, and especially *thinking* than high schools do.

College students are not simply consumers but contributors as well. One obvious way in which you contribute is through active participation in class discussions. When these turn into freewheeling debates, everyone (including the instructor) learns. Just as important are the discussions that students have outside of class. Some will be about history, and even more will use history to support an argument — and fellow students can be very tough critics. Don't look at your peers simply as competitors, though. Reading over others' papers and helping one another in the library benefit both giver and receiver.

It may be that some of you are "draftees," taking the course to fill a requirement, while others are "volunteers," there of your own free will. Any veteran instructor will tell you that the draftees are just as likely to become excellent history students and even history majors as the volunteers are.

Course objectives

These are different from high school, where you got the historical background deemed necessary for good citizenship and in many cases were drilled full of facts in order to raise your Scholastic Aptitude Test scores. A college history course assumes that you have the ability to find out *what* happened in the past. *Why* and *how* it happened, as well as its consequences, require digging deeper. For example, you have known since early grade school that the United States had a civil war. You probably can name at least one of the battles (Gettysburg), state some of the issues (slavery, secession), and possibly give the dates of the war (1861–1865); but you may not yet have made a connection between the Civil War and, for example, seventeenth-century labor problems, the ideology of the American Revolution, and even political strategies in the 1988 elections. You won't be drilled in these things; instead, you will learn to think historically so that you can make the connections yourself. History is not simply a hodgepodge of events occurring in random order. It does make a difference that the Declaration of Independence came before, not after, the Constitution of the United States.

Nor is history just-one-darned-thing-after-another. Writing — and understanding — history requires that we select the relevant facts from among all the things that occur in the past. We know that San Francisco became a great city as a result of the discovery of gold in California in 1848. We also know that the city suffered a bad earthquake in 1906. But that does not mean that gold or even rapid urbanization leads to earthquakes. Nor does it mean that the 1906 earthquake made it certain that another would happen precisely in 1989, although the 1906 event did point up the probability that another would occur at some time. In this case, historical knowledge was translated into building codes that enabled 60,000 World Series fans in Candlestick Park to survive the 1989 quake.

Critical thinking also means that you don't accept without question everything you read or hear. For example, suppose that a tour guide points out a house as a station on the Underground Railroad, a haven for runaway slaves. You, however, notice that a cornerstone or plaque indicates that it was built in 1880. Since you remember that slavery was abolished in 1865, you know that the guide, the plaque, or your own memory must be wrong. It will take further research to find which of the three—if any—is correct. It is the same with lectures, even from famous professors, and textbooks, even by noted scholars. No one is infallible or, indeed, perfectly unbiased. You should always evaluate the information, and you must be particularly careful if it is something that you really want to believe.

The critical skills that you should develop in a history course have applications far beyond the course itself. For example, suppose that you want to open a bike shop and you have an option on a store location. It will pay you to do a little historical research, for if it happens that two bike shops in that location have already failed, you are running a very large risk that history will repeat itself. In this sense, everyone is a historian. That may seem elementary, but an eminent scholar of eighteenth-century intellectual history, Carl Lotus Becker, thought it worth pointing out to professional historians in his 1931 presidential address to the American Historical Association, "Everyman His Own Historian."

The instructor

Your college instructor is a professional historian who has an advanced degree—an M.A. or a Ph.D.—in history, and teaching is just one of his or her many duties. College professors usually teach both an introductory course like the one you are taking and advanced, more specialized courses. For each course, the professor not only gives lectures but also picks the textbook and other readings; makes assignments; conducts discussions (or supervises the teaching assistants who do them); prepares and grades examinations, papers, and workbooks; determines final grades; writes recommendations; and counsels students who want advice. In addition, professors are expected to write books and scholarly articles and to deliver papers at professional historians' meetings. Naturally, they are busy people and very serious about their profession.

Don't let all this intimidate you, however. History professors are willing teachers because they love history and enjoy passing it on to students. They value having you as an audience. They usually are glad to talk to you about points raised in the course, about any problems you may have, and about history and academia in general. However, you should remember that professors are not tutors. They do not have the time to give each student lengthy tutorial sessions, although they will gladly advise you about tutorial services that your college may provide.

Reading

The reading assignments are basic to a college history course. Your professor's lectures are built on the assumption that you already have essential information from your reading. No lecturer wants simply to recite the facts that you need to know. Besides, even seventy-five minutes of rapid-fire lecturing could be printed in just a few pages. The textbook is important because it contains the framework of the course – the chronology and the main figures, movements, and concepts. Instructors may also assign additional readings from books that you are required to purchase or that are placed on reserve in the library. At the introductory level, the reading assignments may be as little as fifty pages a week, but advanced courses will very likely require four times as much.

Some beginning students find a college reading load overwhelming. It's not that they lack reading skills; they simply have never had to exercise them quite so hard. Those of you who are runners or swimmers know how bad it feels when you have gotten out of training, but with practice things soon get easier and then even pleasurable. It works the same way with reading, so hang in there.

In many ways, history is the easiest of disciplines because it is conveyed in narrative form and has little of the specialized terminology that marks other fields. Historians (and their editors) strive for readability because that is one of the hallmarks of a profession that basically concerns itself with glorified story telling. You not only can but should read most history assignments as you would a novel. On the other hand, the study of history does not offer the comfort of a finite number of facts to be memorized. What it does offer is the opportunity to select and connect the facts that will give you a broad, useful understanding of the past. You can, in effect, develop the judgment to be your own historian.

Is there a special way to read history?

Many students find history assignments overwhelming at first: all those pages to cover, all those facts to remember! But you can't memorize history as you would the alphabet or the multiplication tables, and you will suffer great frustration if you try. You can, however, absorb the major propositions in historical writings, and you can remember a surprising amount of evidence ("facts") that support them, if you are systematic. Here are some techniques that will help.

☞ *Lay out a block of time to devote to history.* Start with the assumption that you will need to put in about two hours outside for every hour spent in class; that is, around six hours a week of reading, writing, and reviewing for each three-hour course. Budget your time and, at first, keep track of exactly when you begin and end each session and how much you cover. After a while, you will know whether you work most efficiently with one six-hour session, four hour-and-a-half sessions, or a dozen half-hour sessions.

☞ *Familiarize yourself with the kind of reading you will be doing.* One hundred pages of historical narrative is likely to take less time and effort than twenty pages of a scholarly article or a primary source. (*Primary source* is the historian's term for original documents.) Skim an assignment first to give yourself an idea of the effort it will require.

☞ *Learn to spot the thesis.* This is the most important step of all. Pay particular attention to the first paragraph of each chapter or subheading, because it should contain the *thesis*. A thesis is a proposition whose validity the author demonstrates by presenting evidence. It should come in the first sentence (topic sentence) or the opening paragraph. (Newspapers call this a lead.) You need not agree that the evidence really supports the thesis, but recognizing what the author is trying to prove will make all those facts a great deal more understandable.

☞ *Use a dictionary.* Get in the habit of keeping a dictionary by your side whenever you are reading. Use it whenever you are not absolutely sure of a word's meaning. This is not a sign of weakness; professors are more likely to consult dictionaries than their beginning students are. Your first college book purchase should be one of the several good *collegiate* dictionaries that are on sale in any bookstore for just under twenty dollars — or even less if you look for discounts. Cheaper, usually paperback, dictionaries are useful for spelling and quick definitions, but a collegiate dictionary is easier to use, more durable, and, with its 1500 or more pages, it contains far more information than the smaller and cheaper ones. Especially useful is a collegiate dictionary's section on style, which will answer most of your questions on punctuation, italicization, plurals, and capitalization. Most of them also have a short identification of important persons and geographical names. Before you purchase a dictionary, compare the ones available and pick the one that seems to suit you best.

Studying history is not an exercise in memorization. It is, rather, a process of assembling information from the past and giving meaning to it. For example, let us take this passage from the much-loved textbook by Thomas A. Bailey and David M. Kennedy, *The American Pageant*, 9th ed. (Lexington: D. C. Heath, 1991) 305:

In 1789, when the Constitution was launched, primitive methods of travel were still in use. Waterborne commerce, whether along the coast or on the rivers, was slow, uncertain, and often dangerous. Stagecoaches and wagons lurched over bone-shaking roads. Passengers would be routed out to lay nearby fence rails across muddy stretches, and occasionally horses would drown in muddy pits while wagons sank slowly out of sight.

Cheap and efficient carriers were imperative if raw materials were to be transported to the factories and if the finished product were to be delivered to the consumer. On December 3, 1803, a firm in Providence, Rhode Island, sent a shipment of yarn to a point 60 miles (97 kilometers) away, notifying the purchaser that the consignment could be expected to arrive in "the course of the winter."

There are a number of facts in these two short paragraphs, among them that in 1789 some roads were so muddy that horses drowned in them and that in 1803 a Rhode Island manufacturer could not predict how many months, let alone days, it would take to send a shipment to a customer 60 miles away. But neither of these facts is in itself something one has to memorize. (You will not have to answer an exam question asking, "How long did it take to deliver a shipment of yarn from Providence, Rhode Island, to a point 97 kilometers away in the winter of 1803–1804?" A superintendent of public roads might have the following conversation, but you probably will not. "You think we got potholes? In George Washington's day they had potholes that swallowed a team of horses and the wagon with it! You could look it up.") They are simply rather dramatic examples backing the thesis of these two paragraphs, both of which are evident from the topic sentences of each paragraph: (1) when our nation was new, its transportation system was primitive, slow, and unreliable, and (2) national economic development required that this situation be rectified. On the other hand, neither of these theses would be as memorable without the examples to back them up.

Note also that history studies facts in *context;* that is, in their own time and place. For example, let us consider this sentence from another well-known textbook:

> Because the federal government was reluctant to assert its control over the economy — and because state governments responded only gradually with piecemeal legislation — the job of providing a measure of economic stability fell to American businessmen themselves.

John L. Thomas, who wrote these words (in Bernard Bailyn et al., *The Great Republic,* 4th ed. [Lexington: D. C. Heath, 1992] 2: 95), certainly did not mean that they were true for all periods. Placed in the context of the early years of the Republic or the Progressive or New Deal era, they would be nonsense. The context that Thomas is dealing with is the last three decades of the nineteenth century, and in the next three pages, he makes a convincing case for the validity of his thesis in that particular time.

Historical context is concerned with place as well as time. History textbooks have always contained maps, even before they included other graphic materials, because it is essential for the reader to be "oriented" (literally, to know which way is east). When you began college, you probably went through something called orientation. The maps in a history text serve the same function: to let you know where you are. Whenever you come to a map, stop and examine it. What is its title? (What am I supposed to get out of it?) What is its scale? (How far is it between points?) What kind of map is it? (Does it show physical features, such as mountains and rivers, or does it just have political boundaries?) Thus a study of the map accompanying a discussion of, for example, the battle of Saratoga, will give you a better understanding of why it is considered the turning point in the War for American Independence.

Maps are not the only graphics designed to help you find your way. History texts also use tables, photographs, and graphs, because they convey some kinds of information more quickly and forcefully than do words alone. You can find everyday examples of this in the media: your local daily newspaper, *USA Today*, the *Wall Street Journal*, magazines, and television all rely heavily on graphics to put their stories across. Just as you use maps, you need to pause to determine just what a graphic is supposed to show. It will almost always have a caption that explains why it is there.

On the facing page is an example from a recent textbook that uses both a table and a photograph to illustrate the point that child labor was a serious problem in the late nineteenth and early twentieth centuries. The author could have written a lengthy passage about the large numbers of children in the labor force and the conditions under which they worked—but note how much more economically and forcefully the point is made by the table and picture that follow.

You should also be sure that you know how to interpret the numerical data presented in graphs, which textbooks frequently use. Depending on how they are drawn, graphs either can provide a "snapshot" of numerical data for a single time period—or even a

Children in the Labor Force, 1880–1930

Children gainfully employed, nonagricultural work

Year	Total number of children aged 10–15 (in millions)	Total number of children employed (in millions)	Percentage of children employed
1880	6.6	1.1	16.8
1890	8.3	1.5	18.1
1900	9.6	1.7	18.2
1910	10.8	1.6	15.0
1920	12.5	1.4	11.3
1930	14.3	0.7	4.7

SOURCE: *The Statistical History of the United States from Colonial Times to the Present* (Stamford, Conn.: Fairfield Publishers, 1965).

Young "Spinner-Toter" in a Columbus, Georgia, Textile Mill, 1913. Library of Congress photo; from Paul Boyer et al., *The Enduring Vision: A History of the American People* (Lexington, Mass.: D. C. Heath, 1993) 731.

single moment—or they can show how a quantity changes over time.

The first graph illustrated below (Figure 1), called a bar graph, dramatically shows the great proportional differences in battle deaths suffered by the major combatants in World War I (1914–1918). From the differing lengths of the bars, you can see how much greater were the military casualties incurred in that bloody struggle by Russia, Germany, and France compared to the comparatively small losses of American soldiers and sailors.

"Pie charts" are another kind of graph useful for showing quantitative relationships at one point in time. In Figure 2, for example, the "slices of pie" reveal the proportional contribution of various economic sectors to the total value of U.S. output in 1849. Each sector's share is expressed as a percentage of the total output, and the "pie" as a whole constitutes 100 percent—the entire U.S. economy. Notice how a great deal of precise information is efficiently and clearly conveyed; at least a paragraph would be necessary to say the same thing in words, and it would be much less memorable.

Changes in a quantity or quantity over time can be graphed in a variety of ways. The simplest is a linear graph such as the one shown in Figure 3, which records the growth of the U.S. labor force from

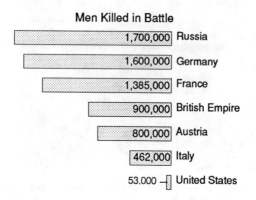

Figure 1. Approximate Comparative Losses in World War I

Thomas A. Bailey and David M. Kennedy, *The American Pageant*, 9th ed. (Lexington: D. C. Heath, 1991) 722.

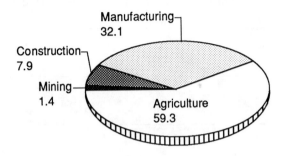

Figure 2. Leading Economic Sectors, 1849

Bailey and Kennedy, Appendix, A27.

1870 to the mid-1980s. Years appear on the horizontal axis, and persons seeking work (in thousands) are indicated on the vertical axis. The rising wavy line charts the actual number who sought work each year. Changes in quantities over time can also be shown through bar graphs, as in Figure 4, a depiction of immigration patterns, 1871–1920. Note that bar graphs allow the author to show decade-by-decade totals, in contrast to the yearly fluctuations recorded by the linear graph.

Most frequently, graphs (like these we have already seen) show either percentages or actual numbers of persons, prices, goods, and the like. But occasionally you will also encounter linear graphs that use "index numbers." An index number measures the degree of change in a quantity (or a group of quantities), starting from a given base year. The quantity for the base year is designated 100. Thus, if the quantity has increased by 10 percent by the next year, the index number rises to 110, and if the quantity declines by 5 percent, the index number drops to 95. Examples of index numbers with which everyone is familiar from newspapers and television news include the Dow Jones average of industrial stock prices and the Consumer Price Index (CPI), which measures the average annual price of a

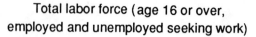

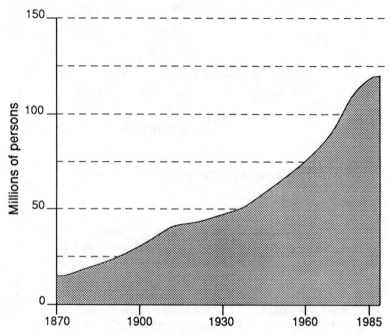

Figure 3. Total U.S. Labor Force, 1870–1990

Bailey and Kennedy, Appendix, A26.

"market basket" of consumer goods, with 1967 prices designated as 100. Figure 5 incorporates both a linear graph of the Consumer Price Index, 1967–1987, *and* a bar graph of annual percentage changes year by year over the same period. The index numbers are indicated on the left-hand vertical axis; the annual percentage changes are measured by the right-hand vertical axis. Using this chart, you can see that in 1980 inflation was running at more than 12 percent annually, and that by 1987 consumer prices had more than tripled in relation to 1967 prices.

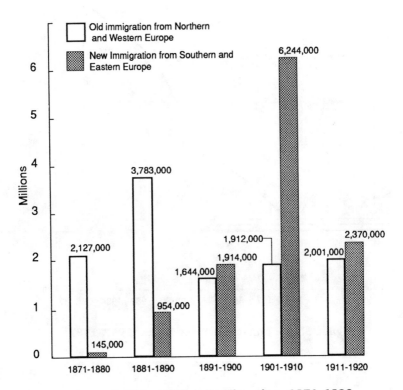

Figure 4. Old and New Immigration, 1871–1920

Bernard Bailyn et al., *The Great Republic*, 3rd ed. (Lexington: D. C. Heath, 1985) 629.

How can I remember all those facts I've read?

Take notes. Abandon any illusions you have about a "photographic memory." You simply will not be able to remember what you have read if you do not write it down. The shortest way to do this is to read through a portion of an assignment (which, depending on the kind of reading and your own attention span, could be anything

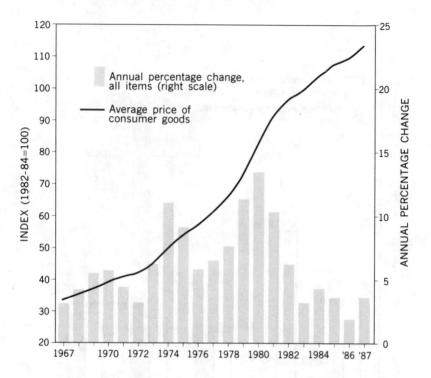

Figure 5. The Consumer Price Index, 1967–1987

Bailey and Kennedy, 968.

from a single heading in a textbook to a whole chapter or even a book), then stop, think about what you have read, and write down in as few words as possible what you think are the author's theses and main pieces of supporting evidence. This procedure will fix them in your mind as well as provide a quick review when you are preparing for an exam.

Increasing numbers of students have started incorporating their reading notes into journals — diaries of their private thoughts. For an excellent essay on this method, see Toby Fulwiler, "Journal Writing in History," in Henry J. Steffens and Mary Jane Dickerson, *Writer's Guide: History* (Lexington: D. C. Heath, 1987) 17–32.

Many students assume that highlighting — that is, underlining or marking words and passages with a pen, pencil, or broad-tipped felt marker — can aid the learning process. Some professors encourage it as well. In theory, highlighting (only of books that you own and plan to keep, of course) affords a quick, easy way to review significant parts of the text: the broad theses, topic sentences, and important passages. In practice, proper highlighting is both slow and difficult for anyone who does not already know a great deal about the topic. For an example of poor highlighting, look at almost any second- or third-hand textbook. It will be filled with underlinings and highlightings of miscellaneous bits of information, usually missing the point. Trying to use such a book is annoying and counterproductive.

If you highlight correctly, you will have to read the assignment through at least twice, marking it only when you go through it a second time. And even then, in the opinion of many professors and experienced students, you will have picked a poor way to digest reading assignments. Here's why:

☞ *It's boring.* Highlighting can turn reading into a mindless marking of dates and proper nouns, which is about as exciting as shelling peas. History is presented in narrative form, much like a novel. Think what marking all the names in *Huckleberry Finn* or *Catcher in the Rye* would do to your enjoyment and understanding of these novels. The marking-pen freaks are often the students most likely to complain about how boring the reading assignments are.

☞ *It can keep you from understanding what you are reading.* It can lift facts out of context, make them meaningless or misleading, and prompt you to write silly exam answers.

☞ *It gets you into the bad habit of defacing books — the library's and your friends' as well as your own.*

☞ *Most of all, it is unnecessary.* Nearly all history textbooks today, and many books of supplemental readings as well, have excellent student guides written by experts who digest themes, list important names and dates, and pose review questions. If you feel that you absolutely cannot read your textbook without highlighting, first consult the student guide for advice on what needs to be stressed.

Taking your own reading notes may seem burdensome at first, but you will find that it is a real time, effort, and sanity saver. Besides, the procedure allows you to record your own thoughts and conclusions.

Do I have to take lecture notes, too?

One of the most obvious ways in which a college history course is different from a high school class is in its use of formal lectures — possibly a throwback to the days when Puritans routinely listened to sermons lasting several hours. Although college lectures seldom go longer than fifty or seventy-five minutes, they are not "sound bites," and they are not relieved by commercials. Getting something out of lectures requires concentration and practice.

Lectures are even harder to remember than readings if you don't take notes; that's why reporters scribble away during press conferences. Although they cannot impart as much information as reading, lectures are essential because they expand, clarify, question, and amend what you have read. (Good lectures will excite or amuse you, too, but that is not their primary function.) Lectures, like reading, require your close attention. Just as you cannot effectively read a history text while watching "Monday Night Football" or "General Hospital," you cannot absorb a lecture while knitting or — worse — completing your assignment for French class. No matter how good your memory, you won't remember a lecture for more than a few hours if you don't take notes. Even if you tape a lecture, you'll still have to take notes on it. (Can you imagine preparing for a final exam by listening to thirty hours of taped lectures?)

Exactly how you take lecture notes is up to you. If you are a beginner, you will need to experiment. Unless you know shorthand, you probably cannot take down a lecture word for word, and you certainly don't need to. People with logical minds can reduce lectures to elaborate outlines. Most of us simply get down as much as we can in some shortened form. Lecture notes can be as idiosyncratic as you please — you are the only one who will have to use them—but make sure that the abbreviations, symbols, and so on will mean something to you days or months later.

☞ *Go over your lecture notes as soon as possible after the lecture.* Some students completely rewrite (and even type) their lecture notes, although most find that unnecessary. Others write commentaries on the lectures in their journals. Probably the most efficient way in which to use notes to fix lectures in your mind is to rule extra-wide left margins (at least two inches) in your lecture notebooks and, when you are going over the notes, use the margin as the place to digest or summarize them. Making these "notes on notes" helps fix the lecture points in your mind and also provides a handy index and review when it comes time to study for exams. Margins are also good places to note dates, references to things you have read, questions, and anything else you think will help you to understand the matter that the lecture covered. In effect, marginal jottings are mini-journals.

Is there a secret for doing well on examinations?

Exams should not be ordeals if you keep up with the reading assignments. Because exams require you to think, preparing for them and taking them are important parts of learning. Examinations also enable the instructor to judge what level of understanding you have attained, which is what grades are all about.

"Objective" exam questions are designed to see if you have done your assignments and grasped the most significant names, events, and concepts. There may be multiple-choice, fill-in-the-blank, and short-definition questions, all of which are efficient ways of testing broadly on your comprehension of the matter you have been assigned. If, after reading an assignment on the colonial period, you should define Cotton Mather as "the most important export of the southern colonies," your instructor will know that you have learned little about Puritanism and southern agriculture alike in the colonial era.

Essay questions are designed to assess how you use historical evidence. They differ from term papers only in the length of time you have to complete them. Any essay, whether it is a one-paragraph short answer, a final-examination question taking perhaps an hour or more, or a take-home exam, should be organized and written just as a term paper. It should start with a thesis and then present the evidence for and against it in a clear, concise way. Stick to your thesis. An essay answer is not a place to dump everything you have learned, whether it is relevant to the question or not.

Most history exams contain a combination of objective and essay questions. The best place to find examples of both is in the student guide that is written to accompany any up-to-date history textbook. The campus bookstore will either have the one for your textbook on sale or can get it for you quickly. Also, it is not only permissible but also wise to try to outguess the instructor. What has been stressed in reading and lectures? What questions would you ask if you were the instructor? How would you answer them? Outline, as briefly as possible, the points you would cover in your answers. Don't feel frustrated if you guess wrong. The practice will do you good, and the information you pick up will be useful — if not for this exam, then for your understanding of history, which is, after all, why you are taking the course.

Well-prepared students nevertheless sometimes do poorly on exams, especially if they fail to keep the following rules in mind.

☞ *Read the instructions.* Make sure that you know exactly what is required. Let's say, for example, that Part I of an exam (25 percent of the total grade) asks you to identify and give the significance of five out of eight items. If you attempt only three, you have lost ten points from the exam (that's a whole letter grade) right there. If you answer all eight, the instructor will probably grade only the first five, even if the last three are absolutely perfect and three out of the first five are abysmal. And if you identify but fail to give the significance, you have flunked 50 percent of that question.

☞ *Budget your time.* If you have 55 minutes for the whole exam and you spend 40 of them on the short-answer section that is worth 25 points, you will have only 15 minutes for the essay questions that are worth 75 points. You will be lucky to eke out a "D" on that test. You will not be given extra time to complete the exam.

☞ *Make sure that you answer the question.* If you write about something other than what is asked, if you wander off the point, or if you fill your answer with facts that may be perfectly correct but are irrelevant to the question, you will probably fail.

☞ *Think before you write.* Organize your answers. For short identifications, ten seconds may be enough. For long essays, ten minutes may be appropriate; use the first two or three minutes to make an outline (which should be cryptic, since you are the only one who will have to understand it) of your answer, in which you propose a thesis and list the main points of evidence. Go over the outline. Add, subtract, reorganize. Then start to write—and write as clearly and correctly as you can, given the constraint of time. Unless so instructed, do not begin by writing down the question; most instructors view that as padding. Start with a thesis statement and end with a conclusion, just as if you were writing a paper.

☞ *If you have time, go over your exam before you hand it in.* Make corrections and additions (easier if you have written on one side only). Do not erase. That takes time and makes everything else hard to read. Draw a single line through anything you want taken out (you don't have to obliterate it—the instructor will ignore anything with a line through it). Do not tear pages out of your exam booklet; some college rules make that an automatic failure for the exam. While few instructors expect perfect spelling and grammar in exam answers, all appreciate evidence that you have tried to catch and correct the more egregious errors.

☞ *After the exam has been marked and returned to you, do not simply look at the grade and throw it away.* Go over it carefully. Read the comments. Look up the objective answers. Re-outline answers to the essay questions. Then, and only then, if you still have questions about the exam, see the instructor. Nothing is less productive (or more annoying to an instructor) than a conference in which a student asks "What did I do wrong?" without having first read over the exam. Keep the exam at least until the course is over. Consult it when you are preparing for the final examination.

The time you spend in attending lectures, in participating in discussions, in reading your assignments, and, above all, in thinking about what you have learned should give you a good basic grounding in history. But there is more to the study of history than that; as one of the liberal arts, history should liberate rather than confine you. In the next chapter we will look at the basic reference books that will let you advance from being a student in an introductory history class to being a scholar who can operate independently.

2. Looking It Up
   and Citing It

Early in your college career you will enter the library—the real center of any institution of higher learning. Many students approach their first visit to the library with unease, possibly because of experiences in school libraries and public libraries. However, most college libraries are quite friendly places, with professional staffs eager to assist. All students of history—senior professors as well as beginning freshmen—must constantly ask questions: an individual must be identified, a date checked, the details of an event examined, the exact wording of a document verified, the meaning of a word established, and so on. You may think that the obvious place to start a search for such historical facts is in the library's catalog, but that is the last place a seasoned researcher goes.

Where do I go first?

The answer you seek may be close at hand, in your textbook (try the index) or your dictionary. (Nothing can make you feel dumber than making a trip to the library in freezing rain to look up something like the exact text of the Fourteenth Amendment to the Constitution and then to discover that it was in your textbook's appendix all along. If this has already happened to you, take comfort in the fact that you are far from alone. It may even have happened to your professor.) But let's assume that you have questions that your textbook cannot answer to your satisfaction.

Most questions like the ones that follow can be answered quickly by turning to appropriate reference books. The reference department of a typical university library may contain almost 40,000 volumes — more than the total collection of many public libraries — nearly every one of which contains information that some curious historian may be seeking.

The following bibliographical essay is an introduction to only a few of the most basic reference books in *general* American history. It does not include, for example, Mark M. Boatner's *Encyclopedia of the American Revolution* or Abby Maria Hemenway's *Vermont Historical Gazetteer,* because these excellent reference works are limited to *specialized* aspects of American history. As you become familiar with your library's reference collection, you will use many such specialized works, but most questions on American history will still be answered by the books listed below. For purposes of demonstration, let us assume that you have come across a reference to the Stamp Act Congress. Most textbooks dealing with the American Revolution mention this meeting, but only briefly. How do you find out more about it?

Note that each reference work has been given an endnote citation to serve as an example of how to cite it correctly in a paper (see pp. 41–44). Read all the endnotes as you come to them, because they contain a wealth of information on both reading and writing such notes.[1]

Where can I look up a historical "fact"?

Dictionaries[2] and encyclopedias[3] of U.S. history

Many reference books are in dictionary form; that is, they list articles or entries in alphabetical order. This format makes the information a lot quicker to find than consulting an index or table of contents for a page number. For example, you can find 120 words under the heading "Stamp Act Congress" in Thomas H. Johnson, *The Oxford Companion to American History* (1966).[4] This handy book also includes biographical sketches of significant Americans — for example, Samuel Adams and Mercy Otis Warren, both of whom played roles in the American resistance to the Stamp Act.[5] (Incidentally, all the *Oxford Companions* are very useful. Depending on the topic, you may want to use the *Oxford Companion to . . .* , for example,

American Literature, English Literature, Ships and the Sea, or *World Sports and Games.*)

A somewhat more sophisticated reference for American history is the *Encyclopedia of American History,* ed. Richard B. Morris, now in its 6th edition (1982). It is *not* in dictionary form, so the user must include page numbers in any citation. Its four parts are "Basic Chronology," "Topical Chronology," "Five Hundred Notable Americans," and "Structure of the Federal Government." Read "How to Use This Book" first.[6] The Stamp Act Congress appears in "Basic Chronology" under the year 1765.[7] "Five Hundred Notable Americans" has entries for "Adams, Samuel," and "Reagan, Ronald [Wilson]," but not for "Warren, Mercy Otis."[8]

A new publication aimed at an audience similar to the *Oxford Companion to American History*'s but 50 percent longer and more up-to-date is *The Reader's Companion to American History,* ed. Eric Foner and John A. Garraty (1991). It has three kinds of entries. Short, unsigned articles, such as one on the Stamp Act, are written by Columbia University doctoral candidates.[9] Longer, interpretive essays on broad subjects such as the American Revolution are written by recognized authorities.[10] Finally, there are signed biographical sketches—for example, for Samuel Adams—though none for Mercy Otis Warren.[11] All the signed essays also include short bibliographies. Each entry is cross-referenced, so that, to illustrate, the long essay by David Brody on "Labor" is cross-referenced with "American Federation of Labor" and "National Labor Relations Act."[12]

For a more complete discussion of the Stamp Act Congress, as well as a basic bibliography on the subject, the well-informed searcher will turn to the eight-volume *Dictionary of American History,* ed. Louise B. Ketz, revised edition (1976). It is one of the few reference works so well known that it may properly be cited, even in a first citation, in shortened form—in this case, as "*DAH,* 1976 ed." (The date is important, because there was a 1940 edition of the *DAH,* edited by James Truslow Adams, that is still in use.) All 7,200 entries are signed by one of the 800 authors who contributed to the *DAH.* The eighth volume contains a very useful index, as well as an errata list (that is, a list of mistakes that nobody caught until after they were printed). You will find about 170 words, plus a short bibliography, on the Stamp Act Congress.[13] The *DAH* also appears in a one-volume abridgment, the *Concise Dictionary of American History* (1983). Entries are unsigned and have no bibliography, but the one-volume version is undoubtedly more convenient and will probably have most of the information you are seeking. In this case, "Stamp Act Congress" is covered in 63 words.[14] Neither version contains biographical entries, since Scribner's has left those to the *Dictionary of American Biography* (q.v. under "Biographies" in this guide).[15]

You need not rely soley on encyclopedias specializing in American history. Do not forget the general encyclopedias that you can find in almost any library and probably learned to use in high school. Any encyclopedias in your library's reference collection are likely to be reliable. Two of the best known and most widely available are *Encyclopedia Americana,* and *New Encyclopaedia Britannica,* (since 1974 known as the *New Encyclopaedia Britannica*). Both the thirty-volume *Americana* and the thirty-two-volume *Britannica* are revised each year, although few libraries buy every yearly issue. For this reason, the date of an encyclopedia is essential. For example, the latest edition of the *Encyclopaedia Britannica,* the fifteenth, was first issued in 1974. All the annual issues since 1974 are still called the fifteenth edition, but each is substantively different in some respects from the others, so most college libraries keep several versions of this edition.

Generally, encyclopedias are arranged alphabetically and are cited like other books that are in dictionary form—that is, by entry rather than by page number. In the sample endnotes for the next two paragraphs, you will note that signed or initialed entries include the author's name, while unsigned entries do not. (*Americana* and *Britannica* have both kinds of entries. To find the author of an initialed entry one must consult a key. In the *New Encyclopaedia Britannica,* this is located in the *Propaedia* volume.) Finally, the *Macropaedia* volumes of the *New Encyclopaedia Britannica* have their own form of citation, because its entries are so long that dictionary form would be inefficient. See for example, the entry for the history of agriculture.[16]

The *Britannica's* idiosyncrasies, such as initialed entries, are partly because it has been around since 1768, and it is still quite English oriented, even though it is now published in Chicago. Try to think of them as charming archaisms, like the wigs British lawyers still wear in court. The *Britannica* is of special interest to history students, because many libraries keep the older editions. These will have a fuller discussion, for example, of an archaic practice like dueling, which gets four pages in the 9th edition (1887),[17] two in the 14th (1973),[18] and only a column in the 15th (1987).[19]

No discussion of encyclopedias useful to history students would be complete without reference to the *International Encyclopedia of the Social Sciences* (1968). It has lengthy, signed entries by international authorities on important concepts in the social sciences.[20] To the original 17 volumes and an index volume, published in 1968, volume 18, the *Biographical Supplement*, was added in 1979. It includes 215 biographies in addition to the 600 in the first 17 volumes. Entries in the *Biographical Supplement* should be cited separately.[21]

Where can I find out what happened on a certain date?

Chronologies

A chronology is a list of significant events arranged by the dates on which they occurred. Chronologies are especially useful when you are trying to put something in historical context. For most purposes, Morris's *Encyclopedia of American History* will be perfectly adequate. However, the most complete and authoritative chronology is the *Encyclopedia of American Facts and Dates,* ed. Gorton Carruth, 8th ed. (1987). Each year is divided into four topical columns — a feature that may be confusing at first, so be sure to read page v for an explanation. The Stamp Act Congress is listed, of course, under the year 1765.[22] You would discover in Carruth that 1765 also saw the opening of the first medical school and first chocolate manufactory in North America, while John Singleton Copley painted a portrait of John Hancock that year, and a Philadelphia teacher advertised that he could teach women to spell.[23] Which of these facts is important depends on the context. You must decide what is relevant for your own purposes.

For more recent events, consult the *Facts on File Yearbook*, which has a heavy emphasis on the United States. Issued weekly since 1941, and bound into well-indexed annual volumes, *Facts on File* lists everything of major importance that has happened on every single day since the beginning of 1941. For example, it carried day-by-day accounts of the Iran-contra arms deal long after the story broke in November 1986.[24] This resource should be cited as a periodical.

How can I find out more about a person?

Biographies

Since history records the activities of people, the biographical volumes of a reference department are as important to the scholar as are the history volumes. They are so frequently used that everyone who reads books with footnotes is expected to know what the initials *DAB* and *DNB* stand for. The *Dictionary of American Biography*, almost always cited as *DAB*, was originally published in twenty volumes between 1927 and 1937. Most libraries have the ten-volume reissue published in 1964, which contains the original twenty volumes, Supplements 1 and 2, and an index. To this have been added (so far) Supplements 3 to 8 and a *Complete Index Guide* (1981). The *DAB*'s British prototype is the *Dictionary of National Biography*. Commonly known as the *DNB*, it was originally published in 63 volumes and 8 supplements between 1885 and 1900. If you are dealing with the colonial period of American history, many of your subjects may be English or Scottish persons who can be found only in the *DNB*.

Citing the *DAB* may seem difficult at first, but the task becomes easy when you have learned its idiosyncrasies. The *DAB* has lengthy (one to ten pages), signed biographical sketches of deceased persons who lived in the United States. In the original volumes and early supplements, following the British practice inherited from the *En-*

cyclopaedia Britannica and *DNB,* each entry was initialed by the authority who wrote it. Proper citation requires giving the author's name, which must be translated from a key in the front of each volume: for example, "L. P." is Louise Pound, who wrote the entry on Helen Hunt Jackson.

Note that because the 1964 version is the two-volumes-in-one reissue, there are *two* keys in each book, one of them in the middle. Make sure that you use the right one. Since the *DAB* is, of course, in dictionary form, you should not give the volume number; but if the entry is from one of the supplements, do cite the supplement number.[25] For example, Helen Hunt Jackson appears in the first twenty volumes because she died before 1927.[26] John Foster Dulles died in 1959, so he is in Supplement 6, covering Americans who died between 1956 and 1960.[27] President Lyndon Johnson is an example of a famous, dead American who is not yet in the *DAB* because his death in 1973 was too late for Supplement 8 (1988), which covers 1966–1970. Until issue of Supplement 9, one must look for Johnson in another place — for example, in the *New York Times Biographical Service,* in *Current Biography,* or in one of the general encyclopedias discussed above.

For many purposes, you may find shorter sketches adequate. The *DAB* through 1960 has been abridged as the *Concise Dictionary of American Biography,* 3rd ed. (1980). The entries are unsigned.[28]

Magnificent as they are, the *DAB* and *DNB* are very male oriented. For women in American history who died before 1951, consult the three-volume *Notable American Women, 1607–1950,* ed. Edward T. James (1976). Biographies of 442 American women who died between 1951 and 1975 are in *Notable American Women: The Modern Period,* ed. Barbara Sicherman and Carol Hurd Green (1980). All entries are signed and should be cited just as for the *DAB.* Note, however, that scholarly convention has not yet awarded *Notable American Women* the sensible short title of *NAW* as a counterpart of *DAB, DNB,* and *DAH.* It is permissible to strike a blow for both equal rights and convenience by noting in your first citation of *Notable American Women* that it will be "[hereafter *NAW]*" in the rest of your paper. As examples in our endnotes here, suppose we were citing the entries for Mercy Otis Warren[29] and Ethel Rosenberg.[30]

Frances Trollope is an example of someone who is not included in the *DAB* or *Notable American Women,* because, although as author of *Domestic Manners of the Americans* (1832) she was a noted observer of the American scene, she remained proudly English. She is important enough, however, to have gained admission to the virtual men's club of the *DNB*.[31]

Two of the most useful sources for recent lives are periodicals, each with monthly issues that are then collected as annual volumes. *Current Biography* has been printed ever since 1940; it includes most of the people who have made big news since then. For example, knowing that President Johnson died in 1973, one would look up his obituary notice in *Current Biography* 34 (1973) and find there that the last full sketch appeared in *Current Biography* 25 (1964), which would list not only earlier sketches in *Current Biography* but also all other sources used in compiling the sketch. *Current Biography* is in dictionary form, and its entries are unsigned.[32]

The other periodical is the *New York Times Biographical Service,* published monthly since 1972 and collected in annual binders. It is a collection of clippings from the *New York Times* about people in the news, and it is much more convenient than cranking through the microfilm copies of the *New York Times.* *New York Times Biographical Service* should be considered a monthly magazine for citation purposes.[33]

☞ *Tip:* Scholars seeking authoritative biographical information know that the *New York Times* publishes extensive obituaries of noteworthy people. These are prepared long in advance and constantly updated, so that, for example, on January 23, 1973, the day after former president Lyndon Johnson died, the *New York Times* printed an enormous obituary—it ran twenty pages when it was reprinted in the *New York Times Biographical Service*.[34]

If the person whom you are trying to find is too recent or obscure for the *DAB* and the other sources mentioned above, see if your library has the *Biography and Genealogy Master Index,* 2nd ed. (1980–1985), or, better yet, the microfiche version, *Biobase,* which is updated annually. These list everyone who has ever appeared in a biographical collection, including some of your own ancestors and most college faculty members, and tell where you can find biographical sketches of them.

There are a great many other biographical collections, some of them highly specialized, such as a 10-volume work devoted to mountain men and fur traders.[35]

CAUTION: a large part of many libraries' biography section is occupied by the impressive green volumes of the *National Cyclopedia of American Biography*. You should leave these alone for now. The *National Cyclopedia of American Biography* is useful for trained researchers in demography and genealogy, but it is not an authoritative source for historical biography.

How can I locate a historic place?

Atlases and gazetteers

Your library will have atlases (books of maps) and gazetteers (dictionaries of place names) for nearly every area and subject, but the beginning American history student will probably find the following adequate. For gazetteers, the handy *Webster's New Geographical Dictionary* (1984) has 47,000 place names.[36] The more cumbersome *Columbia Lippincott Gazetteer of the World*, ed. Leon E. Seltzer (1952), comprises 130,000 place names and basic information about them.[37]

Most reference departments contain a bewildering array of atlases in several different locations (since atlases tend to be oversized), but the handiest general atlas of United States history is the *Atlas of American History*, ed. W. Kirk Reynolds, 2nd rev. ed. (1984), issued as a companion volume to the *Dictionary of American History* (q.v.).[38] For economic history, look first at the *Historical Atlas of the United States*, ed. Clifford L. Lord and Elizabeth H. Lord (1953).[39]

Atlases are cited as books, except that maps are often cited by plate number rather than by page.

Where do I find figures on topics like literacy and commerce?

Historical statistics

The U.S. Census Bureau has collected statistical data about our country since 1790. For the United States Bicentennial, it issued *Historical Statistics of the United States, Colonial Times to 1970,* which incorporates English colonial material all the way back to the early seventeenth century. If you are interested in the progress of American education, *Historical Statistics* would show, for instance, that in 1870, 20 percent of Americans over age ten were illiterate. In the next thirty years, the number fell to less than 11 percent, and by 1969 only 1 percent of Americans could not read and write.[40]

Where do I find the exact text of a historical document?

Primary sources

These documents are the raw materials of history. Consulting primary sources is essential in preparing a term paper and useful even when you are just reading an assignment. Some collections of primary sources run to hundreds of volumes. The following, however, should answer most of your needs. For example, you can find the text of the Resolutions of the Stamp Act Congress, along with an informative introduction and brief bibliography, in *Documents of American History,* ed. Henry Steele Commager, 9th ed. (1973).[41] Serious students of American history may want to buy a personal copy of Commager's *Documents,* which is also available in paperback.

A much larger collection of documents that is very popular with term-paper writers, especially if they are looking for longer and less political documents than most of those in Commager, is the twenty-three-volume (to date) *Annals of America,* ed. Charles Van Doren (1968–1977), which includes twenty volumes of American history documents through 1976.[42] Each source has an introduction and a biographical sketch of the author. It happens that *Annals of America* also contains the Resolutions of the Stamp Act Congress, but this does not mean that *Annals* duplicates everything in Commager's *Documents. Annals* is especially useful for researching a paper because it also includes an index volume and two "Conspectus" volumes.[43]

This book calls Teddy Roosevelt gay. Does that mean what I think it does?

Language dictionaries

No, it doesn't. Words may have different meanings at different times in history. There are many English-language dictionaries throughout the library. Be sure to consult one of them whenever you are not certain about what a word means. Especially when you are dealing with primary sources, it is essential that you know what a word meant at a particular time. For example, *memorial* was once used as *memorandum* is today. If a writer in the 1770s calls John Hancock condescending or one in the 1930s describes Theodore Roosevelt or Franklin D. Roosevelt as gay, do not leap to conclusions based on your knowledge of usage in 1990. Turn to a dictionary of historical principles, which traces changes in forms and meanings of a word through time. The greatest of these is the *Oxford English Dictionary,* commonly called the *OED.*[44] The first edition, originally issued in ten volumes from 1888 to 1928, took fifty-four years to produce, and almost half of its 15,487 pages were written by Sir James Murray, in consultation with thousands of English-language experts around the world.[45] Most college libraries have the 13-volume 1933 edition and the four supplements issued 1972–1986. The *OED* was, however, very English. Therefore, Murray's co-editor, Sir William A. Craigie, brought out *A Dictionary of American English* (1938) on purely American usage. It is usually cited as *DAE.*[46] Craigie has been

supplemented by *A Dictionary of Americanisms on Historical Principles,* edited by Mitford M. Mathews (1951).[47]
In 1989 the second edition of the *OED* came out. It is a good deal more transatlantic than the 1933 edition, incorporating Craigie's and Mathews's Americanisms and even adding some that they do not have. For instance, the 1989 *OED* lists not only lists "Vermontese" and "Vermonter" but also "Vermonteer," which was not in Craigie or Mathews. (It also has slang and "dirty" words which were eschewed by the very Victorian original *OED*, even if they had a good deal of historical usage.) If your library has the 1989 *OED*, by all means use it, although the 1933 edition will always be serviceable.

Browsing through the library's dictionary shelf will reveal many dictionaries of specialized language, including volumes covering "soldier talk," slang, euphemisms, recently coined words, and so on. As long as the entries are in alphabetical order, they should be cited in dictionary form.[48]

I have to find six books and scholarly (whatever that may mean) articles — two of them published since 1975 — on the Emancipation Proclamation before class tomorrow. Help!

Bibliographies

It's easier than you think. The first place to look for authoritative works on any aspect of American history is the *Harvard Guide to American History,* ed. Frank Freidel, rev. ed., 2 vols. (1974). Volume one is arranged topically; volume two, chronologically. Since you know the Emancipation Proclamation came during the Civil War, 1861–1865, you turn to the Civil War part of the second volume and there, under the heading "Emancipation" (section 46.10.2), you will find eight items.[49] Among them are a book by John Hope Franklin, *Emancipation Proclamation* (1963), and an article by Lorraine A. Williams, "Northern Intellectual Reaction to Emancipation," *Journal of Negro History* 46 (1961): 174. The *Harvard Guide* also lists a number of the people involved. To find books about these individuals, you would consult the biography section in the first volume.[50]

The *Harvard Guide,* however, lists nothing published after June 30, 1970. To find what has been written more recently about American history, consult *America: History and Life: A Guide to Periodical Literature,* a periodical published since 1964. It is especially useful because it abstracts (that is, has short digests of) articles from 2100 different journals, making it much easier for a student to decide if an article is worth consulting. As the discussion below will demonstrate, *AHL* (as it is usually cited) is a bit tricky to use. It helps to consult "User's Guide" at the beginning of each annual volume.

AHL began with a retrospective volume covering articles published 1954–1963. Volumes 1–10 (1964–73), issued four times a year, consisted only of article abstracts and citations, with the fourth number being a subject and personal names index for the first three numbers. Volumes 11–25 (1974–88) had seven issues a year. Three of them were called *AHL Part A, Article Abstracts and Citations,* and were an expanded version of the old *AHL. AHL Part B, Index to Book Reviews* came out twice a year. It listed all the scholarly reviews of books on American history for the year. *AHL Part C, American History Index (Books, Articles, and Dissertations)* was an annual formal listing of all the articles and books in Parts A and B, plus all doctoral dissertations in American history for the previous year. Finally, *AHL Part D, Annual Index,* was an expanded and cross-referenced subject and author index for the other three parts. Beginning with volume 26 (1989), *AHL* was simplified to five issues. The first four numbers all contain article abstracts, book review listings, dissertation citations, and, for the first time, citations of film and video reviews and reviews of works on microfilm/fiche. The fifth number is the cumulative index for the whole year.

The annual index, whether Part D or number 5, is the place to start your search. For example, under "Emancipation Proclamation" you would find "15A:993," meaning that you turn to item 993 in Part A of volume 15 (1978). Listed there is an article by Herman Belz, "Protection of Personal Liberty in Republican Emancipation Legislation of 1862," *Journal of Southern History* 42(1976):385–400. The abstract shows you that it is what you are looking for.

CAUTION: A comprehensive search will take a lot of time, though *AHL's* five-year indexes certainly help.

☞ Do not try to search for scholarly articles in *Readers' Guide to Periodical Literature.* This resource, with which you are probably familiar, lists only magazines intended for the general public. It would not, for example, have a reference for the article by Belz in *Journal of Southern History.* You are looking for articles that have met the exacting standards of the historical profession.

CAUTION: *America: History and Life* puts the publication data for periodicals in an unusual format that is not used by the historical profession. When you are making citations or bibliography ("bib") cards (discussed in Chapter 3), you must follow the order authorized by *MLA* and *Chicago* (discussed below under "Style manuals"). Note, for example, this entry from the 1986 *AHL:*

23C: 2257
Voigt, David Q. FROM CHADWICK TO THE CHIPMUNKS. *Journal of American Culture 1985 7(3): 31–37.* 23A: 447.

The proper form for citing the item above in an endnote is:

David Q. Voigt, "From Chadwick to the Chipmunks," *Journal of American Culture* 7.3 (1985): 31–37.

Using *America: History and Life* is not easy, particularly the first time you try it, but it is still the quickest and most comprehensive way to find the latest publications on any aspect of American history.

Reference departments also have literally hundreds of bibliographies on specialized subjects such as the American Revolution, the Civil War, and African-American history. One specialized bibliography useful for paper writing is the *Guide to American Foreign Relations Since 1800*, ed. Richard D. Burns (1983). It defines foreign relations very broadly and provides not only lists but also abstracts, or summaries, of books and journal articles. Reading the abstracts will save you time by letting you know whether a book or article is likely to have what you are looking for.

Can I do any of this by computer?

Online, disc, and microform searches

In the future, bibliographic searches may be handled almost exclusively by computers. A computerized system offers the great advantage that the "database" can be updated as soon as new publications come out. Furthermore, computer searches are faster and sometimes more reliable than going through the printed volumes. But they require fairly sophisticated thinking on the part of the searcher. This is probably best acquired by slogging through the old printed bibliographies discussed above, which will help you to understand what the computer does in microseconds and thus give you a better idea of the kinds of questions to ask it.

Your library may already subscribe to two kinds of computer-search facilities. "Disc" refers to services such as Wilson Disc, which distribute compact discs that are usually updated at regular intervals, often four times a year.[51] "Online" services are those that come from a computer connected to your terminal by telephone wires and whose databases are constantly updated. Online services usually charge a substantial fee for each use.

CAUTION: The papers that you write during your first two years of college are unlikely to need the comprehensive coverage of a subject that a computer search can give you. Fifteen pages of bibliography printouts are not what you want when the paper itself is supposed to be six pages long. Besides, computer searches usually suffer from the same disadvantage as subject searches in a library catalog: they tell everything that has been written without letting you know what is good, bad, or even relevant to your particular needs. You can rely on the items listed in the *Harvard Guide*, and you can at least read the annotations in *America: History and Life*. Still, if you are curious and are willing to take the orientation instruction that most libraries require before you can start computer searching, go ahead and give it a try.

A special consideration for historians is that most computer databases have only the most recent publications. This is seldom a problem for the sciences, where material quickly becomes outdated, but it is crippling for historical research. If your library subscribes to the online-search service "Knowledge Index," you can use it to search *America: History and Life* since 1964. ABC-Clio, the publisher of *AHL*, is now also bringing out a disc version that is somewhat easier to use than the printed one. Check to see if your library gets it. Wilson Disc issues a Humanities Index, which includes all important history journals. It also issues a Social Science Index, which is sometimes useful to historians who need information from political science, economics, sociology, geography, or anthropology journals, but it has no journals commonly considered "historical." (*Reader's Guide* is also available on disc and online, but, as noted above, it is of limited use for most history papers.) More online services will surely become available to students in the future. Consult with the person in charge of your library's search terminals.

Some services, among them "Nexus," give a whole article, not just the citation for it. As yet, however, they are too expensive for most college libraries. In addition, some of the standard reference works, such as encyclopedias, language dictionaries, and thesauruses, can now be searched by computer, and more are being added all the time. There is nothing wrong with availing yourself of such aids, as long as you don't depend on them to do your thinking. Treat computer printouts with the same skepticism that a scholar treats all evidence.

Finally, there are still many bibliographies and other research aids that are on film, requiring use of microfilm, microcard, or microfiche readers. Among them is the *National Newspaper Index*, which indexes on microfilm approximately the past three years of five leading U.S. newspapers: the *New York Times, Washington Post, Los Angeles Times, Wall Street Journal,* and *Christian Science Monitor.* This index is updated monthly and is quite easy to use if you follow the instructions printed on the reader. *National Newspaper Index* is also available on optical disk, which is read from a computer terminal. Ask a reference librarian whether your library has one of these versions. Storage problems have led most libraries to keep college catalogs, government documents, newspapers, and some journals on microfilm, microcard, or microfiche rather than in their original paper form. Someday, resources like these may be kept in computers rather than on film. In the meantime, take care to follow instructions when you use microforms; they are fragile.

Is there a resource that tells me the correct way to do footnotes and things like that?

Style manuals

A scholarly paper—including any student term paper—should be presented in a style accepted by the discipline. Your library's reference department will have many different style manuals covering all disciplines.

Journals and other publications in history, as well as most of the other humanities, almost always specify the use of either "MLA" or "Chicago" for their authors. These guides are, respectively, the Modern Language Association of America's *MLA Handbook* and the University of Chicago Press's *Chicago Manual of Style.* While quite similar, the two styles advanced in these manuals are not interchangeable. Your instructor either will specify one of these or will leave the choice up to you.

Most reference departments have multiple copies of the *MLA Handbook for Writers of Research Papers,* ed. Joseph Gibaldi and Walter S. Achtert, 3rd ed. (New York: Modern Language Association, 1988), because so many different disciplines use it.[52] You may run across several versions of the *MLA.* The first edition (1977, white cover) is obsolete, although many guides to historical study and writing still follow it. The second edition (1984, black cover) had major changes from its predecessor. It discarded most of the conventions that seemed needless, annoying, and time consuming in the 1977 version, and it is still usable, though not as clear or "fine tuned" as its successor.

The third edition of the *MLA* (1988, silver cover) is state of the art. If you are given a choice of styles, *MLA* may be the most practical option. It is required by most departments in the modern languages, so you will probably use it for your English and foreign language courses, as well as for those in some of the other social sciences and humanities. Most of my own students have opted for *MLA,* and so it is the form I have followed for the citations in this guide.

CAUTION: *MLA* stresses the "parenthetical documentation and list of works cited" method of citation (sections 5.2–5.7). At this time, no historical journals and few history classes accept this method. Most history papers require endnotes that refer to superscripted numbers (raised slightly, like this[1]) in the text of the paper. If you use *MLA,* be sure to follow the method in section 5.8, "Using notes for documentation."

Chicago Manual of Style, 13th ed. (Chicago: University of Chicago Press, 1982), has the advantage of being the accepted style guide for the major historical journals, including *American Historical Review* and *Journal of American History.* For this reason, many history departments require *Chicago* for graduate students' term papers and theses. *Chicago* is the oldest and probably the most widely used of the style guides, but it is very comprehensive and rather expensive. Library reference departments often have only a single copy. At one time it was accompanied by a cheap, reliable, undergraduate student's exposition, the late Kate L. Turabian's *Student's Guide for Writing College Papers* (1976). However, Turabian's guide bears little resemblance to the 1982 edition of *Chicago Manual of Style*. Your library will probably have copies of the 1976 "Turabian," but if you use it you will be learning an out-of-date style. Unfortunately, therefore, it cannot be recommended unless a new edition comes out.

Recently, the University of Chicago Press did bring out a fifth edition, revised and expanded by Bonnie Birtwistle Honigsblum, of Turabian's *A Manual for Writers of Term Papers, Theses, and Dissertations* (Chicago: University of Chicago Press, 1987). It is a godsend for graduate students and thesis writers, but most undergraduates will probably find this manual harder to use than *MLA*. Still, it is useful for students who aspire to be professional historians.

An especially good style manual for those who want to follow *Chicago* style is William G. Campbell, Stephen V. Ballou, and Carole Slade, *Form and Style: Theses, Reports, Term Papers*, 8th ed. (Boston: Houghton Mifflin, 1990). "Campbell," as it is commonly known, has in this edition used *MLA* for examples of parenthetical citations and *Chicago* for footnote/endnote citations. Campbell's examples are far more comprehensive than those in either *MLA* or Turabian's *Manual for Writers*. Campbell also has the best examples of proper format for papers and theses that I have seen. When in doubt about any matter of form, you can usually find the answer in Campbell.

Now am I ready to go to the catalog?

Your stop in the reference department may have answered all your questions, but more likely it has simply prepared you to go on to the library's main collection of books and periodicals. Now you are indeed ready to consult the catalog.

Only a few years ago, the catalog was a series of cabinets with drawers containing cards filed in alphabetical order by author, title, and subject. Each card included a call number, usually from a standard system like the Library of Congress system or the Dewey

Decimal system. This number enabled you to request books or to find them yourself if you had access to the stacks. Your library may still use a card catalog, but in recent years, more and more libraries have converted to online computer catalogs and at the same time have changed to Library of Congress call numbers.

Online library catalogs are marvelous time savers, but they are very unforgiving. You must follow directions and spellings exactly, or the catalog will disclaim all knowledge of books that you know the library has. For more directions on how to use an online catalog, see the next chapter, page 49.

If your library is "open stack" — that is, you are allowed to go directly to the shelves — use the call numbers to find the books that you want to consult. Your library will have a plan or directory that tells you which floors to go to. If the library is not open stack, you must put author, title, and call number on each request slip. When looking for periodicals, be sure to note from the catalog which ones are shelved alphabetically and which are on microfilm, usually stored alphabetically in cabinets.

Follow the library's rules! Don't try to help by returning books to the shelves, because, however well meaning, it often results in books that are misplaced and thus lost to other users. If you run across a misshelved volume, put it on a table or cart where the library staff can take it to its proper home and perhaps check it off a "missing" list. And never, ever, mark in a library book.

Library research may be used for many things — even for settling bets (history departments and library reference departments get a lot of calls from people doing just that). Most of your questions, however, will probably come up in the course of writing papers. That is the subject of the next chapter.

Endnotes

[1]The following endnotes are cited according to the form in Joseph Gibaldi and Walter S. Achtert, *MLA Handbook for Writers of Research Papers,* 3rd ed. (New York: MLA, 1988) section 5.8, which is discussed below under "Style manuals." The abbreviation *e.g.* in the following endnotes means "for example" (Latin, *exempli gratia*). Your dictionary or a style manual will give the meaning of any unfamiliar abbreviations.

[2]"Dictionary" is defined as "a reference book listing alphabetically terms or names important to a particular subject or activity along with discussion of their meanings and applications." *Webster's Ninth New Collegiate Dictionary,* 1985 ed. Some familiar reference works, including *Webster's Collegiate Dictionary, Encyclopaedia Britannica,* and *Dictionary of American History,* commonly are cited with only the year of the edition and omit the number of the edition itself.

[3]"Encyclopedia" or "encyclopaedia" is "a work that contains information on all branches of knowledge or treats comprehensively a particular branch of knowledge, usu. in articles arranged alphabetically often by subject." *Webster's,* 1985 ed.

[4]Thomas H. Johnson, "Stamp Act Congress," *Oxford Companion to American History* (New York: Oxford UP, 1966). Note that Johnson is the *author* of this work, whereas most reference books will have an *editor.*

[5]Johnson, "Adams, Samuel" and "Warren, Mercy Otis." (Note that this is a subsequent citation of a work already cited, and thus does not repeat all the information of the initial citation. In this case the author alone is enough, since no other books by Johnson have been cited. Note also that when citing an entry from a book arranged in dictionary form, you should give the entry *exactly* as it appears; that is, you will find "Stamp Act Congress" under "S" but "Adams, Samuel" under "A".)

[6]*Encyclopedia of American History,* ed. Richard B. Morris, 6th ed. (New York: Harper, 1982) xi–xiv. This is a good book for your personal library.

[7]*Encyc. Am. Hist.* 88. This is a subsequent reference to the work cited above in note 6. Therefore, it does not repeat all the information required for a first reference, and the title may be abbreviated, as long as it is clear to what work you are referring.

[8]*Encyc. Am. Hist.* 972, 1135–36.

[9]"Stamp Act," *Reader's Companion to American History,* ed. Eric Foner and John A. Garraty (Boston: Houghton Mifflin, 1991). Because the book is in dictionary form, the citation does not need page numbers, and since this particular entry is unsigned, no author is cited.

[10]Richard L. Bushman, "Revolution," *Reader's Companion.*

[11]Richard D. Brown, "Adams, Samuel," *Reader's Companion*. Although there is no entry for Mercy Warren, the index reveals that she does appear in Abraham S. Eisenstadt, "History and Historians," *Reader's Companion* 500–501. In this case the page number needs to be cited, because Mrs. Warren is only a small part of a long essay.

[12]This requires no citation, since all the information necessary to find the entries is already in the text.

[13]Winfred T. Root, "Stamp Act Congress," *DAH*, 1976 ed.

[14]"Stamp Act Crisis," *Concise DAH*, 1983 ed.

[15]*Q.v.* is a Latin abbreviation that constantly appears in reference works. It is short for *quod vide* (literally, "which see"), meaning that further information is available under that heading. In this case, turn to "Biographies" in this guide.

[16]Eric S. Higgs, "History of Agriculture," *New Encyclopaedia Britannica: Macropaedia*, 1987 ed., 13:185:2a. (Translation: vol. 13, p. 185, top half of second column. The author is listed only as "E.S.H.," so one has to find those initials in the *Propaedia*.)

But for the 1982 edition the correct citation is: Eric S. Higgs, "Agriculture, History of," *New Encyclopedia Britannica: Macropaedia*, 1982 ed., 1:325e. Note that both the 1982 edition and the 1987 edition are designated "15th edition," yet the title of the article by Higgs was changed from "Agriculture, History of " (1982) to "History of Agriculture" (1987). Furthermore, the system both of numbering volumes and of locating an item on the page was also changed, although the article is the same, and the reference in both cases means the top part of the second column of a page in the first volume of the *Macropaedia*. That is why you must always give the year.

[17]Francis Storr, "Duel," *Encyclopaedia Britannica*, 1887 ed.

[18]Charles-Louis de Beaumont, "Duel," *Encyc. Brit.*, 1973 ed.

[19]"Duel," *New Encyc. Brit: Micropaedia*, 1987 ed.

[20]For example, Mario Einaudi, "Fascism," *International Encyclopedia of the Social Sciences*, 1968 ed. Note: since the articles are long (this one is eight pages), specific references—for example, to quotes—should usually include a page number.

[21]For example, John Higham, "Beard, Charles A.," *Int. Enc. Soc. Sci.: Biographical Supp.*

[22]*Encyclopedia of American Facts and Dates*, ed. Gorton Carruth, 8th ed. (New York: Harper, 1987) 80.

[23]*Encyc. Am. Facts and Dates,* 78–81.

[24]"American Hostage Freed in Lebanon; Secret U.S.–Iran Arms Deal Revealed," *Facts on File* 46 (Nov. 7, 1986): 825–26; "Reagan Fields Questions on Iran Arms Policy," *Facts on File* 47 (March 20, 1987): 175–78.

[25]The *MLA,* up to the 1984 edition, required that the date of the particular sketch be included but is now silent on the matter. There now seems no good reason to bother with this frankly exasperating task.

[26]Louise Pound, "Jackson, Helen Maria Fisk Hunt," *DAB.* Note that the title of the entry must be given exactly as it appears in the *DAB.* A specific citation could also include a page number.

[27]Lloyd C. Gardner, "Dulles, John Foster," *DAB,* Supp. 6.

[28]E.g., "Adams, John Quincy," *Concise DAB,* 1980 ed.

[29]Robert A. Freer, "Warren, Mercy Otis," *Notable American Women* [hereafter *NAW*] (Cambridge: Harvard UP, 1971).

[30]Carol Hurd Green, "Rosenburg, Ethel Greenglass," *NAW: Mod. Per.* (1980).

[31]Richard Garnett, "Trollope, Frances," *DNB.*

[32]E.g., "Jackson, Michael," *Current Biography* 44 (1983).

[33]E.g., Jon Pareles, "Michael Jackson at 25: A Musical Phenomenon," *New York Times Biographical Service,* Jan. 1984: 74–75.

[34]*New York Times Biographical Service,* Jan. 1973, 81–100.

[35]Since this work is not in dictionary form, it must be cited as a multivolume book: e.g., Cornelius M. Ismert, "James Bridger," *Mountain Men and the Fur Trade,* ed. Leroy R. Hafen, 10 vols. (Glendale, CA: Clark, 1965–72) 6: 85–104.

[36]"Burlington" in *Webster's New Geographical Dictionary,* 1984 ed., lists thirteen cities and towns, of which the one in Vermont is number 10.

[37]"Burlington" in *Columbia Lippincott Gazetteer of the World,* 1952 ed., has eighteen American cities and towns by that name, plus separate entries for "Burlington, Ontario," and "Burlington County, NJ."

[38]E.g., "Burgoyne's Invasion, 1777," *Atlas of American History,* ed. W. Kirk Reynolds, 2nd rev. ed. (New York: Scribner's, 1984) 84.

[39]E.g., "Corn Production, 1840," *Historical Atlas of the United States,* ed. Clifford L. Lord and Elizabeth H. Lord, rev. ed. (1953; reprint New York: Johnson, 1972) plate 101.

[40]*Historical Statistics of the United States, Colonial Times to 1970,* 2 vols. (Washington, D.C.: U.S. Bureau of Census, 1975) 1:382.

[41]"Resolutions of the Stamp Act Congress, October 19, 1765," *Documents of American History,* ed. Henry Steele Commager, 9th ed., 2 vols. (Englewood Cliffs, NJ: Prentice, 1973) 1:57–58.

[42]*Annals of America,* ed. Charles Van Doren, 23 vols. (Chicago: Encyclopaedia Britannica, 1968–77) 2:158–59.

[43]A conspectus is an overview. In this case, it is a topical index, not only of the *Annals* itself, but also of American history. *Annals of America* 21:xx.

[44]E.g., "Memorial," *OED,* reveals the now obsolete meaning of "a note or memorandum" as early as 1577 and as late as 1827.

[45]An excellent description of the process is Michael Olmert, "Points of Origin," *Smithsonian* 13(August 1982):34–37.

[46]E.g., "Yankee," *DAE.*

[47]E.g., "Vermonter" was used to denote a resident of Vermont as early as 1778, while "Vermontese" meant the same thing between 1783 and 1845. *Dictionary of Americanisms on Historical Principles,* ed. Mitford M. Mathews, 2 vols. (Chicago: U of Chicago P, 1951).

[48]E.g., "grunt: 1. (Pre–World War II)s. [slang] An Army Signal Corps assistant. 2. (Vietnam to Modern)s. An infantryman." John R. Elting, *A Dictionary of Soldier Talk* (New York: Scribner's, 1984). Complete publication data are given in this example because this specialized dictionary is not as well known as, for example, *Webster's.* Note how essential the historical context is for the meaning of this word: a grunt mentioned in a soldier's letter written in 1918 would refer to something different than in a letter written in 1968. Incidentally, this usage appears in the second, but not the first, edition of the *OED:* "**grunt,** sb., [definition 2b] *U.S. slang.* An infantry soldier." *OED,* 1989 ed.

[49]*Harvard Guide to American History,* ed. Frank Freidel, rev. ed., 2 vols. (Cambridge: Harvard UP, 1974) 2:858–59.

[50]*Harvard Guide,* 1: 156–274, alphabetically arranged. E.g., p. 156 shows six items for "Adams, Abigail," and three for "Adams, Samuel."

[51]Current convention uses *disc* to refer to CD-ROM ("compact disc – read only memory") and *disk* to refer to "floppy" diskettes.

[52]The Modern Language Association also publishes the *MLA Style Manual* (New York: MLA, 1985) but, outside of some added chapters on publishing, it appears to be identical to the *MLA Handbook.*

3. Writing Book Reviews and Papers

Rather than relying on English composition courses to do the job, more and more colleges are using survey courses in such disciplines as history as a means of teaching writing. If your first U.S. history course assigns book reports or term papers, this chapter will provide guidance. In addition, reading it over will enhance your understanding of history and the process by which it is written. The description will also give you a preview of what is in store in more advanced courses.

For many students, the most frightening part of a history course is writing papers. That is a pity, for writing a paper affords the best opportunity that you will have to express yourself, to propose your own ideas in light of your historical training. Solving the puzzles presented by a term paper will also give you an appreciation of historical research and writing. Most important, writing is the one skill gained in a history course that is most likely to pay off in the "real world." Academia has no monopoly on the written word; a corporation's standards for research and writing are at least as high as a university's. Former students frequently tell professors how their training from term-paper assignments got them jobs and promotions.

The process of writing a paper should be the same for freshmen, advanced and graduate students, and professors. The difference between a three-page paper and one ten times as long is mostly in the preparation time. The steps outlined in the following discussion may look like overkill for beginners, but they are not. Eliminating such steps as bibliography cards, notes, and rough drafts will cost more time and effort than it will save, and it will result in much poorer papers.

The first rule is to get started early. The deadline will loom almost before you know it, and a paper cobbled together without adequate thought will not only embarrass you but do violence to your grade. If you give yourself enough time, writing a paper can even be an enjoyable experience.

Does a book review count as a paper?

In many history classes, the first written exercise is a book review, typically between 200 and 800 words (one to four typewritten pages). It provides a transition from the techniques for taking reading notes (described in Chapter 1) to those for writing a research paper (discussed below).

The reading notes that you take for yourself are a form of book review. In them you identified the source, told what kind of reading it was (text, article, primary source, and so on), and, most important, identified the thesis and listed the main points backing it. You may even have commented on what you found good, bad, or puzzling about it. However, you are the only one who must understand your reading notes. In contrast, a book review done as a class assignment has an audience of the instructor and possibly your fellow students, so it must be presented more formally. The process of getting it into final form is much the same as that discussed below for research papers, particularly in the sections on rough drafts and the final copy. Rewriting is especially important in book reviews, because they are so short that every word must count.

The elements and organization of a book review usually are as follows:

1. the heading, which includes author, title, and publication information;

2. the opening paragraph, which includes a brief summary of the book and especially its thesis;

3. a recap of the evidence that the author uses to back the thesis (a discussion of the author's point of view may be part of this summary);

4. a discussion of how the book supports, attacks, modifies, or expands the view of a subject covered by the course;

5. comments about the book's readability and any features, such as illustrations and bibliography, worthy of note;

6. a final recommendation for or against the book as an aid to understanding the subject.

You can get some idea of how book reviews are written by looking in scholarly journals like the *Journal of American History* and *The Historian,* or those intended for nonprofessionals, such as *Newsweek, Harper's,* or the *New York Times.* Note that they are well-constructed essays that impart a lot of information in a few words. You should try to emulate their readability and terseness (rambling on is the sin student book reviewers are most likely to commit). Remember, however, that scholarly journal reviews are written by and for professional historians with a wide knowledge of the subject. *Your* context is the course you are taking: the lectures, textbook, and other readings. The book reviews in magazines and newspapers, on the other hand, are more like movie reviews: they are less concerned with imparting information than with suggesting why the general public should purchase or ignore the item being reviewed. Your report must do more than this.

For a fuller discussion of how to write book reports, see "Reviewing books and articles" in Henry J. Steffens and Mary Jane Dickerson, *Writer's Guide: History* (Lexington: D. C. Heath, 1987) 60–68.

How do I choose a paper topic?

In an introductory course, the topic may be picked for you. Usually this is in the form of a thesis or proposition; for example, "Once he became president, Thomas Jefferson proved to be more 'federalist' than the Federalists." Your task is to canvass the evidence for and against the proposition and to present a clear, cogent argument for or against its validity. There is no right or wrong answer to such a proposition, but there are certainly good and bad uses of evidence, and convincing or unconvincing arguments.

If the topic is up to you, keep in mind that there are limits to your choice. For example, if the course begins with the year 1877, you may not write about the Civil War (though it is part of U.S. history). For the same reason, you could not expect a course on Shakespeare to accept a paper on the Federal Reserve System (even if Shakespeare did discuss money lending in several plays). When in doubt, ask the instructor about your choice.

Select a topic from a research area that you think you will enjoy. Keep "paper topic" in mind when you are reading and listening to lectures, and make a note whenever you spot something that you would like to pursue further. Do not be too concerned about "significance" — dress styles, games, and gardening are just as worthy of your attention as wars and politics are. Furthermore, material evidence like buildings, tools, and household furnishings may tell as much about the past as literary evidence such as newspapers, letters, and memoirs, and both must pass the same exacting tests for reliability. Scholars should be skeptics, particularly about things they want to believe.

Choosing the final paper topic is largely a matter of paring down. You might start with a topic like "Expansion," but that is obviously too large for a term paper. "Transmississippi Expansion" or even "The Settlement of the Middle West" is still too big for most papers, although either would be a reasonable place to start your search for a topic. After dipping into one or two sources or doing some background reading, you might then come up with "The First Settlers in Minnesota," which ought to be a manageable paper topic. Once started on your research, you might decide that what really interests you (or what you have the most information about) is the way newcomers reacted to the unfamiliar prairie environment. Or the trail might lead you out of the flatlands to a paper on what the mountain men ate. Feel free to modify a topic or even abandon it and replace it with something entirely different; professional historians do so all the time. Remember, the earlier you start, the more opportunity you will have to make changes.

How do I do research on a historical topic?

Begin with the general and work toward the specific. The best place to start is with your textbook. It provides the historical context for your paper, and its bibliographies will recommend important works on various topics. When you move on to the library, go first to the reference collection. Look up key words, people, and places in the standard reference works—*Dictionary of American History, Dictionary of American Biography,* chronologies, encyclopedias, and gazetteers—discussed in Chapter 2. Many will have cross references and bibliographies that will lead you further. Consult standard bibliographies such as *Harvard Guide to American History* and *America: History and Life.* Check the collections of primary sources, like Commager's *Documents of American History* and Van Doren's *Annals of America,* for pertinent documents.

After you have done your preliminary digging in the reference section, it is time to go to the library catalog. Use its cards or on-line screens to find which of the books you found in the bibliographies are in your library's collection. On both cards and screen you can find them by either author or title—check both if the first doesn't bear fruit, because library catalogs are not infallible. If you are using an online catalog, you also have the option of "keyword" search, which is very handy if you don't know the exact title.

Catalogs also list "Library of Congress Subject Heading" cards or screens. Librarians love these, but beginners should avoid them for now. To use the LCSH correctly, one must first consult the three enormous, red volumes the Library of Congress compiles annually (the 1991 edition has nearly 5000 pages). Even then, what you will get is a list of all the books related to a particular topic and its cousins, with none of the selection and annotation you get from the bibliographies in the reference collection. When you get to an advanced level, a librarian will be glad to introduce you to the mysteries of the LCSH.

Remember also that the library catalog will not contain journal articles (which you must find in bibliographies), but it will tell you whether the journal itself is in your library's collection.

CAUTION: It is, believe it or not, quite possible to overdo the research part of a paper. Nailing down the last little fact, waiting for a book to be called in, spending too much time researching a topic's background — activities like these are often used as excuses to delay the moment when you have to start writing. Worse, papers that never get to the point often result. If you have any doubt about how much research is reasonable, talk to the instructor.

From the very beginning of your research, make bibliography cards and notes. Otherwise, you will find yourself frantically searching your memory for where you found something. Even for items that turn out to have no application to your paper, it is worth making bibliography cards, because you may find use for them in another context.

Why all the bother about bibliography cards? How are they going to help me?

The first step in writing a paper is to assemble a bibliography. Bibliography cards (almost always called bib cards) are just about the greatest labor-saving device that a writer has. Done right, bib cards keep, in a quickly retrievable and flexible form, all the information you need for making proper citations and bibliographies. They are essential adjuncts to your reading and research notes and provide a personal reading record.

You should never go into a library without a packet of 3" × 5" cards with which to make bib cards. Learn to make them immediately and correctly; if you copy information into a notebook and later onto bib cards, you double the time, the effort, and especially the opportunity to make errors. The task really is easiest if you take pains to get it right the first time.

You can make bib cards from bibliographies like *Harvard Guide* and *America: History and Life,* from book reviews and advertisements, from footnotes and chapter bibliographies, and from library catalogs, as well as from the books and articles themselves. Take pains to be precise, for a bib card with misspellings or incorrect information is worse than none at all. For example, make sure that all information appears in the right order, and indicate when the person on the top line is the editor or compiler rather than the author.

A useful bib card must contain, in correct order, all the information required for a proper citation; that is, author (or editor or compiler), title, publication data, and all other pertinent items listed in standard style sheets such as the *Chicago Manual of Style* and the *MLA Handbook.* Layout and order are even more important than legibility. Figure 1 on the following page is an example of the minimum bib card.

☞ *The bib card is a standard-size index card.* Always use 3" × 5", because you will not need anything bigger. Index cards last longer and are easier to shuffle than slips of paper. The cards may be either lined or unlined, though lines are convenient.

☞ *Each card is done in ink (though some people type their bib cards), for permanence.*

☞ *The information is arranged for speediest use:*

1. On the topmost line and all the way to the left is the author, with last name first so that the card can be filed alphabetically by author. (If there is no author, title should go on the top line). **CAUTION:** Don't number your bib cards. You are going to have a lot more of them before you are through, and you should file them all together in alphabetical order.

2. On the next line or lines comes the title. When there is a subtitle (indicated by a colon), it is included, as in Figure 1, even though it is not always necessary to include the subtitle in a citation. Note that the title is not underlined (though it will be when you use it in a proper citation) because the location on the card tells you that it is a title.

3. The publication data follows, on a new line. The example in Figure 1 includes the edition only because it is not the first; first editions should not be so identified.

That is all you really must have. However, bib cards are a good place to keep other useful information as well. Consider the card in Figure 2 on page 54.

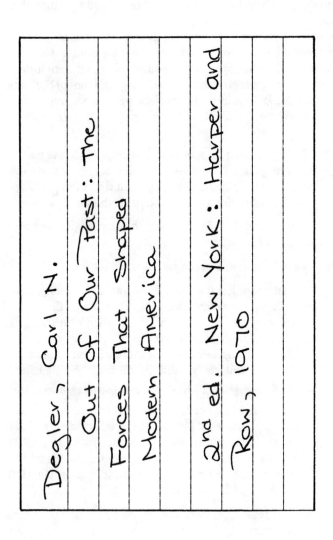

Degler, Carl N. Out of Our Past: The Forces That Shaped Modern America. 2nd ed. New York: Harper and Row, 1970

Figure 1.

Note that the essential information appears in the top three lines. The lower part of the card records some features of the book that the bib-card maker thought might be useful later: photographs from the 1880s, examples of oral history, first-person accounts by women, and so on. Note especially the call number. Jotting it down can save a lot of time, for you won't have to run back to the catalog if you want to find the book again.

In the case of bib cards (though not reading and research notes), if you need more room you may put additional information on the back, such as how you made use of the book, where you found out about it (for example, *Harv. Guide* 427 or *AHL* 12A: 2137), other works to compare, reviews, and strengths and weaknesses. These notes will be invaluable when you write bibliographical essays and annotated bibliographies.

Bib cards for periodical articles should follow the periodical-citation form of your style sheet (such as *MLA Handbook,* 3rd ed. [1988], 191–94). Note that periodicals are not cited the same way as books. They do not, for example, give place and publisher. Figure 3 on page 55 shows a rather complete bib card for a periodical article.

Because this is your card, you know that *JAH* stands for *Journal of American History,* and, since the *JAH* has continuous pagination, you omit number and month from the data line. Note that the card gives library location (Microform Room) and brief comments, including the fact that you found a reference to this article in *America: History and Life.*

If you do them correctly, your bib cards will save loads of time and trouble:

You will need to do endnotes only once — for the final version of your papers — rather than copying them over and over.

You will need only the briefest identification on research notes and marginal notes of rough drafts — just enough to get you to the right bib card.

You will be able to write without having books in front of you — essential when the library is closed and your paper is due at 8:00 A.M.

Stratton, Joanna L.

Pioneer Women: Voices from the Kansas Frontier

New York: Simon and Schuster, 1981

Intro by Arthur M. Schlesinger Jr. Pp.320. Bib, index, photos, endpaper map, appendix, guide to L.D. Monroe Coll. Pioneer stories, but no citations. Interviews in 1920s of KS frontier women ca. 1850-1890. Top. arr. Good fwd.

HQ/1438/.K2/577

Figure 2.

Williams, David
"The Bureau of Investigation and Its Critics, 1919-1921:
The Origins of Federal Political Surveillance"
<u>JAH</u> 68 (1981): 560-79
Documents failure of fed. restriction on FBI-
type agencies. Scary. Cf. Monkkonen.
MICRO   AHL   19A: 7761

Figure 3.

What is the best way to take research notes?

Having chosen your research materials and made bib cards for them, you are now ready to read them and take research notes. Many historians' experience lies behind the following suggestions on note taking.

☞ *Treat research notes, like bib cards, as permanent, not as simply useful for a single assignment or course.* You will be surprised at how often material that you looked up for a paper on, for example, Renaissance art will prove handy in an entirely different context. Do your research notes as if you expected to need them next year. To start with, use paper that is not "erasable," and make your notes with a typewriter or in ink. (If your library forbids ink, spray your penciled notes later with artists' fixative.)

☞ *Keep notes on cards or slips of a convenient, standard size.* Cards are durable and come in standard 3" × 5", 4" × 6", and 5" × 8" sizes. They are also expensive, heavy, and bulky. Paper slips, either from pads or homemade, are perfectly adequate. The size is up to you, but it is one you must settle on and stick with. 4" × 6" and 5" × 8" sizes are popular because they are widely available in the form of index cards and note pads, and they fit in file boxes and accordian files. 5 1/2" × 8 1/2" size is also popular because it is cheap and convenient: one merely cuts in half a standard sheet of typing or looseleaf paper, tablet, old memos, or outdated letterhead. Printing on the back is no problem because you are going to use only one side. (Make sure, however, that your cut is straight.) The great disadvantage is that no one seems to manufacture 5 1/2" × 8 1/2" files. If you make your own slips, be sure that you get them right. You don't want to be stuck forever with notes that are 4 7/8" × 5 3/16". You have to be able to file and shuffle them with your other notes. Sometimes you will need to take notes on whatever is at hand. Recopy them later onto standard-sized slips. Photocopying is a quick way of doing this.

CAUTION: Copying information into your notebook and later onto a note card or a bib card not only takes twice as much time but also doubles the chance to make errors. It really is easier and more accurate to make the card at once and then check it while the catalog, title page, or whatever is in front of you.

☞ *Write on one side only.* Otherwise, inevitably that bit of vital information you know you have somewhere will always be on the other side.

☞ *Put quotation marks around all direct quotes.* Make a solemn pact with yourself that everything without quotation marks is either a paraphrase or a summary. Nothing is more frustrating than having to guess from your notes whether a neat phrase is somebody else's (which in your paper would have to be put in quotation marks) or your own (which would not, although the original source still must be cited).

☞ *Whenever you are copying word for word, copy exactly and use quotation marks.* Carefully read over both the original and your note; they must be identical. Never, for example, use an abbreviation that is not in the original, and never spell out a word that is abbreviated in the original. If you omit anything, so indicate with ellipsis points (three . . . spaced dots, not . . .). If you add anything not in the original, put it in [square brackets] (not parentheses). If your typewriter doesn't have square brackets, fill them in with your pen.

CAUTION: Photocopying is a sure way to get quotes exactly right, and it can often save time. Its great disadvantage is that some students seem to think that photocopying is a substitute for reading the material. You will still need to make at least rudimentary notes about the material to keep track of what you have, and you'll still need to think about what it means.

☞ *Learn to paraphrase and summarize.* Not only will your papers be better (most students' papers have too many direct quotes), but you will save a lot of nickels and time standing in the photocopier line.

Paraphrases are restatements of someone else's words, ideas, or information in your own words, but they nevertheless require citation of source. Many notes are a combination of direct quotes and paraphrase. You must use quotation marks to show which is which.

Summaries put information in the most concise form. If a note is from one of your own books, such as a textbook, it may be no more than a reminder of where to look up the original.

☞ *Except for direct quotes, be as idiosyncratic as you wish in taking research notes.* Strange abbreviations, shorthand, slang, jargon—all are permissible if they work for you in summarizing accurately. Just remember that you might have to understand them again, in another context.

☞ *Put headings on your note cards that will make sense ten years from now.* They should allow you quickly to identify what is in the note and which bib card to use for a quick citation. They include both a subject heading and a bibliographic heading. It doesn't matter whether you put subject on the left and bibliography on the right or the other way around, just as long as you do all of your cards the same way.

Subject headings should be detailed enough to give you a good idea of each note's contents as you flip rapidly through your files. Obviously, "Civil War" will be too general if you are searching for information on Admiral David Farragut at Mobile. Good subject headings are an art developed through practice.

Bibliographic headings should include just enough to lead you to the proper bib card. Usually the last name of the author and a short title plus page numbers should do the job.

Figures 4 and 5 on the following two pages show a bib card, a research note, and a proper endnote made from them.

Stinchcomb, William

"Talleyrand and the American Negotiations of 1797-1798."

JAH, 62 (1975): 575-90

MICRO

Figure 4. Bibliography card (3" × 5")

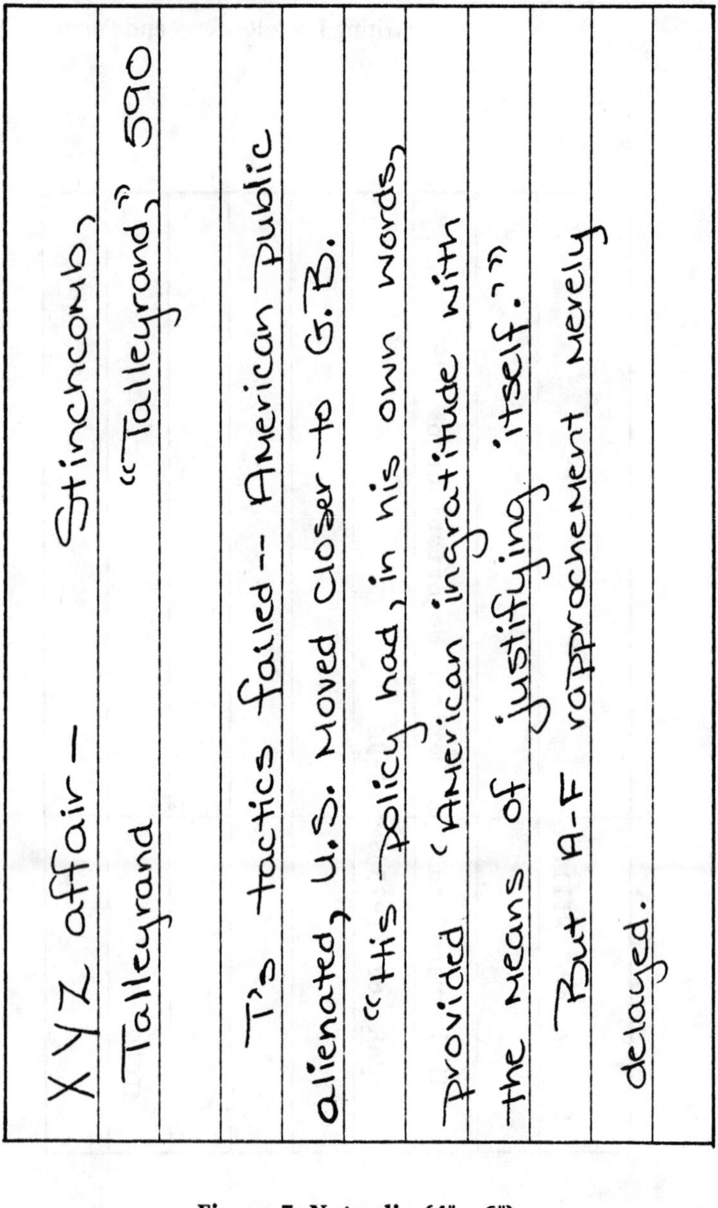

XYZ affair — Stinchcomb,
Talleyrand "Talleyrand," 590

T's tactics failed — American public
alienated, U.S. moved closer to G.B.

"His policy had, in his own words,
provided 'American ingratitude with
the means of justifying 'itself.'"

But A-F rapprochement merely
delayed.

Figure 5. Note slip (4" × 6")

[1]William Stinchcomb, "Talleyrand and the American Negotiations of 1797–1798," *Jour. Am. Hist.* 62 (1975): 590.

CAUTION: Don't fall victim to these common beginners' mistakes:

1. not taking research notes at all, but trying to write papers out of a welter of books and photocopies;

2. keeping research notes in notebooks rather than on loose slips (a procedure that could necessitate note slips to guide you through your notebooks!);

3. putting too much on each note slip;

4. writing on the back;

5. using odd shapes and sizes of paper and even using them vertically rather than horizontally;

6. devising inadequate headings, such as shortcut numbering systems that will serve for only one paper;

7. failing to copy direct quotes exactly;

8. quoting where a paraphrase or summary would be better;

9. throwing away notes at the end of the assignment, class, or year.

How do I turn my bib cards and research notes into a paper?

Now that you have done your research, read over your notes. Sort them into piles that seem to make organizational sense. This requires space — a clean desk or table, a bed, the floor — and lots of thought. Whenever a thesis — that is, what you think the evidence seems to prove — suggests itself, write it down: for example, "Mountain men ate as much fat as they could get." You may have many theses, some of which you will quickly discard. Don't agonize too much over this part. You're just beginning, and your final thesis will have gone through many modifications.

At this point, some writers are ready to construct an outline. Others need to overcome inertia by starting to write with no particular organization or attention to choice of words or the niceties of spelling and grammar, simply letting thoughts flow onto paper or screen for ten minutes or so. If you use this approach, read over your first thoughts, discarding whatever seems irrelevant. You may want to repeat the process several times, until you have a good idea of where you're going. Then you make an outline before settling down to the real first draft. (For a discussion of this "free writing" approach, see Peter Elbow, *Writing Without Teachers* [New York: Oxford UP, 1973].)

Whenever you prepare an outline, start with your thesis (the statement of what your paper will demonstrate), followed by the evidence that will prove your point. Some scholars write very complete outlines; others use a personal shorthand meaningless to anyone else. Experiment first with the complete outline, but ultimately do whatever works for you.

I have to make a rough draft? Can't I get it right the first time?

No, you can't, even if you have a very comprehensive outline. For one thing, nothing is more inhibiting to a writer than the knowledge that this is the version that will be handed in. You don't need that anxiety. For another, first drafts almost always contain extraneous matter. The secret of good writing is rewriting, and that most definitely includes cutting.

Using your thesis statement and outline as a road map, write the first draft of your paper. Proceed in any way that feels comfortable to you: with a pencil, pen, typewriter, word processor, lined or unlined paper, legal or letter size, backs of old memos, whatever. Even if they know how to touch-type, many people find that they compose best with a pencil or pen in hand. Evelyn Waugh always wrote his novels with a fountain pen, while Truman Capote found inspiration in lots of sharp pencils. When asked what word-processing program he used, *New York Times* computer columnist Eric Sandberg-Diment confessed that he wrote with a ball-point pen on a legal pad. John Updike composes his novels and stories on an electric typewriter but does his *New Yorker* book reviews on a word processor. James Reston has for over half a century turned out *New*

York Times columns and stories using only two fingers and a manual typewriter, while most of his fellow journalists have joyfully embraced the computer. Experiment. What works for you is right. There really are only two rules for rough drafts. Unless you are using a word processor, be sure to follow them.

☞ *Give yourself plenty of room.* Paper is much cheaper than your time. The more space you leave for additions, corrections, citations, and notes to yourself, the more useful and economical the rough draft will be. Perhaps you will find it helpful to draw a wide margin — say, 2 ½" — on the left, so that you will have plenty of room for additions, corrections, and citations (pending their becoming actual endnotes). Use wide lines. Some set their typewriters on triple-space, as in this example,

though others find that double-space leaves enough room for

corrections. If you compose on a word processor, be sure to

print out a rough draft in double-space, because you will

probably pick up things from the printed copy that escaped

you on the screen.

☞ *Write on one side only.* Using both sides may save a few cents in paper, but it will cost you a fortune in time and potential mistakes. The easiest way to reorganize a paper is simply to cut it apart and tape the pieces together in a different order. This is impossible if you have written on both sides. Usually you will want to rewrite some parts of a draft but not others. Remember, the more times you recopy a quote, the more chance for errors to creep in.

Cite your sources even in the earliest and roughest draft; don't wait until the final copy to put in citations. If you write your drafts by hand, on a typewriter, or on a computer whose word-processing program does not have automatic footnoting, the best way to keep track of citations is to put them in parentheses within the text, so that the citations will go along with blocks of text when you cut and paste. Don't number citations until you are ready to convert the rough draft into the finished paper, because you will be adding, subtracting, and moving text. The last step on your final rough draft is to mark citation numbers in colored ink. Then, using your bib cards, you need to do your endnotes only once, for the finished paper. This trick alone will save much time and trouble.

If you compose on a computer with a program that has automatic footnoting, by all means use the feature. Whenever you make a change, it will automatically renumber the notes. You may want to put citations at the bottom of the page for rough drafts, then instruct your computer to put them at the end of the final paper.

A WORD ABOUT COMPUTERS. In the first edition of this booklet, I observed that "many people have found writing on a word processor easier and more conducive to creativity than any other way because making changes is so easy. . . ." Now, only three years later, using a computer is less a choice than an imperative for college students. Most college libraries have gone "on line," so that you must use a keyboard even to consult the catalog. Employers expect college graduates to have word-processing skills, and now many college instructors do, also. Fortunately, most of you have been introduced to computers at an early age (unlike senior professors, many of whom did not even know how to type before libraries removed their old card catalogs, and were nonplussed at the necessity of learning the keyboard).

If you somehow escaped the computer so far, your college almost certainly provides training. Take advantage of this. Self-teaching is the toughest way to learn about computers, and trying to write a paper with an unfamiliar computer or word-processing program is courting disaster. Furthermore, instructors have become increasingly unlikely to accept the "unfamiliarity" excuse for papers that are late or improperly formatted. Don't risk learning on the job. Make your first effort a letter home, not an assignment you'll be graded on.

Colleges usually have terminals and personal computers, complete with word-processing programs, for students to use — though the competition for them may be fierce. They also often have deals that enable you to acquire your own computer and word-processing program far cheaper than you could anywhere else, even at the big electronic discount houses. If you cannot afford a new computer even at college prices, look around for used ones. It does not take a state-of-the-art computer to do word processing. If you are in the market for a computer, check to see if your campus is committed to a particular system, such as Macintosh or MS-DOS. Now that IBM and Macintosh can speak to each other, this makes less difference than it once did, but some campuses and academic programs may still require a particular operating system. [1] Some instructors already require that work be submitted on disk, and this will probably become common in a few years.

Choice of a word-processing program is as important as choosing a computer. There are now dozens of programs, but not all of them are created equal. The cheapest, easiest to learn, and simplest are little more than glorified electric typewriters. Many of these elementary programs are available as part of a business package or even as shareware. They are useful, but you will soon wish for something more. At the top of the scale are expensive, powerful programs designed for mass mailing and desk-top publishing, features you will not need for writing academic papers. (On the other hand, the publishers of these monsters often offer them to college students at enormous discounts, on the assumption that you are the executives of the future. Be sure to check with your computer center or bookstore for such deals.) Your minimum requirement should be a program that will do footnotes/endnotes and automatically renumber them when you make revisions. It must also have a spelling checker, though this feature, along with grammar checkers, dictionaries, thesauruses, etc., can usually be added separately. And print preview is becoming a necessity, not a luxury.

I urge you to purchase your own word-processing program. I know that software piracy is nearly universal, but if you acquire a program legally you will also get the instruction books, a number to call when you run into trouble, useful newsletters, and free or discounted upgrades. Besides, using other people's software is the surest way of getting viruses.

Writing with a computer is different—and easier—than any other way. You can keep files of notes and bibliographies in your computer and let it copy them into your paper. You need not worry about making typing mistakes, since they can be corrected instantly. With a couple of keystrokes, you can move whole blocks of text around—and any citations will be automatically relocated and renumbered. Spelling and grammar checkers make proofreading far less onerous than it is in a handwritten or typed paper, though they will not write the paper for you, nor will they catch misinformation and improperly used words. With a computer, you can do all your editing on the screen, printing only the final version. Still, it is advisable to print out at least one rough draft, for most people seem to catch things in print that they miss on a screen. And remember that Murphy's Law[2] applies equally (make that *especially*) to computers, so save frequently and make backups on another disk at the end of every session with your computer.

However you compose your rough draft—pen, pencil, typewriter, or computer—read it over several times. Make changes. Scribble on it. Cut it apart and tape it together in a different order if need be. A useful rough draft ought to look pretty messy before you have finished with it. As a matter of fact, a professional writer's rough drafts generally look messier than a beginner's.[3] Keep asking yourself:

☞ *Does what I have written support my thesis?* If it does not, you should reformulate the thesis. Don't be surprised if the last revision you make is a rewrite of the first paragraph. Don't alter the evidence to fit the thesis.

☞ *Are things in the right order?* Background material may be important to your paper, but your readers don't want to wade through it before they find out what the paper is about. Many first paragraphs ought instead to come second. Furthermore, presentation of evidence should be in a logical order, and what looked logical in the outline may, when written, demand relocation. (Here is where you'll be thankful that writing only on one side lets you use scissors and tape.)

☞ *Is every item necessary?* If not, cut it out. Be ruthless. It hurts to delete an amusing or striking anecdote, but if it is not directly relevant to your thesis, it must be killed. Another excellent reason for keeping your notes is that you may find a use for such an anecdote later.

☞ *Is any direct quotation, particularly a long one, really essential?* Could you not make the point at least as well in your own words? A paper that is merely a collection of other people's words is both boring and a cop-out. Words seldom "speak for themselves." Remember, however, that you must still give credit for a fact or idea even if you have expressed it in your own words. Failure to cite the source for any ideas, information, or turns of phrase not your own constitutes the crime of plagiarism. Plagiarism is one of the most serious offenses against academic honesty, carrying penalties from failure on a particular paper to dismissal from the college or university.

How do I avoid plagiarism?

Plagiarism originally meant "kidnapping." To *plagiarize* is "to steal and use (the ideas or writings of another) as one's own" (*American Heritage Dictionary,* 1969 ed.). There is a particularly good discussion of plagiarism, complete with examples, in section 1.6 of the *MLA Handbook,* 3rd ed. (1988), 21–25. In addition, your college or university will have its own statement on plagiarism, probably in the student handbook under "Academic Honesty."

☞ *Deliberate plagiarism.* This is copying or paraphrasing someone else's work, whether a published book or article or a term paper. It is comparatively rare, though far too many ex-college students are waiting table or pumping gas because they committed this crime. You may be tempted by the thought that "Professor X will never know that I took this from a 1922 *American Historical Review.* This topic is not in his specialty. Besides, I won't copy it word for word." *Forget it.* Professor X may be unable to remember the names of his own children, but he has an uncanny ability to detect phrases and ideas not your own — and even identify their source — faster than you can copy them. Don't risk it. The stakes are too high. (The computer also offers a temptation to plagiarize. *Forget that, too.* Professors can spot computer-generated plagiarism just as easily as they can the old-fashioned kind. Furthermore, software is already on the market that claims to be able to detect "98 percent of term-paper plagiarism."[4])

☞ *Inadvertent plagiarism.* Without realizing it, you may have committed large chunks of others' words to your memory and then written them down as your own. If you have not given a citation, you are *really* in the soup. The best way to avoid this is to keep decent research notes and, whenever in doubt, to look again at the original source. Remember, you must give a citation for every fact and idea unless it is (a) general knowledge or (b) your personal observation or thought. More on this later.

☞ *Ignorant plagiarism.* This is a result of not knowing the rules. In spite of all the statements on plagiarism like those above, some students still think that only direct quotes must have citations. This misinformation leads to both massive overuse of quotations and failure to give credit where it is required.

When in doubt, give a citation. While it is not required that you cite a source for something that is common knowledge, such as the fact that the Union won the battle of Gettysburg in July 1863, it is far better to receive a gentle reminder that you are perhaps overdoing your citations than it is to have your margins filled with large, angry, red demands for **SOURCE?!** or to receive a summons to an academic-honesty hearing.

What are the rules of citation?

What to cite

The rules of citation require careful attention and practice. Review the discussion of plagiarism above. The following list from Joan H. Garrett-Goodyear et al., *Writing Papers: A Handbook for Students at Smith College,* rev. ed. (1981) 37, is an excellent guide to what must be cited:

1. all word-for-word quotations (except common sayings)
2. all passages that you have summarized or paraphrased
3. all charts, graphs, and diagrams that are not your own
4. all statistics that you have not compiled yourself
5. all theories or interpretations that are not your own
6. all key words or terms that you have taken from a specific source

How to cite

Choose an accepted citation style, such as *Chicago* or *MLA.* The examples here follow the form in the *MLA Handbook,* 3rd ed. (1988), section 5.8.

For most history term papers, as for any material submitted to an editor for publication, the acceptable form of citation is the endnote. Endnotes are exactly what they sound like: they come at the end of your paper, not at the bottom of the page. **(CAUTION:** *Footnote* is often used as a generic term for all kinds of citation, so don't be fooled.) Endnotes are always double-spaced. They begin on a new page after the last text page of your paper, and the endnote pages continue the page numbering of your paper. Endnotes give the source of items that have been reference marked by a superscript number in the text of the paper.

In general, documentation requires the following:

☞ *Who the author of your source is.* This not only gives credit where it is due but also allows your reader to judge the reputation of your source. For example, Gordon Wood has a certain standing among authorities on the American Revolution, David Donald on the Civil War, and Arthur Link on Woodrow Wilson.

☞ *Where the information can be found.* This means including at least a title, plus other information that will allow your reader to find the source quickly.

☞ *When your source was written.* It makes a great deal of difference to a sophisticated reader whether your information comes from 1927 or 1983. Give the original date of the edition that you are using, not the copyright renewal; and if you are citing a reprint, provide both the original date and the date of the reprint. For example:

[2]Brooks Adams, *The Emancipation of Massachusetts* (1887; rpt. Boston: Houghton, 1962) 237–38

The original date reveals the context in which Adams wrote about Puritan New England. He was not an eyewitness, nor did he have the advantage of the scholarship of such modern authorities as Bernard Bailyn, Perry Miller, Samuel Eliot Morison, or Edmund S. Morgan.

☞ *Location within the work:* that is, volume, page, section — whatever is necessary to find the source.

☞ *Place of publication and the publisher.* These are less essential to your reader, and some styles (though not the ones acceptable for most courses) omit one or both. You should omit the publisher of works published before 1900.

If you have made proper bib cards, you will not have to run off to the library to find publication information in the midst of typing the final copy.

☞ *Special procedure for periodicals.* Periodical citations are different from those for books. They do not, for example, give place or publisher. You should consult the style manual you have decided on, such as *MLA* (section 5.8.6), for details on how to cite different types of periodicals. However, in general the information is as follows:

1. author's name, followed by a comma
2. title of the article, enclosed in quotation marks and followed by a comma
3. title of the journal itself, underlined
4. the number of the volume
5. the year of publication, in parentheses and followed by a colon
6. the page numbers. For example:

[1]Robert E. McGlone, "Rescripting a Troubled Past: John Brown's Family and the Harpers Ferry Conspiracy," *Journal of American History* 75 (1989): 1179–1200.

☞ *Subsequent citations.* Once you have given the first citation of a source, subsequent references to it should furnish only the minimum information necessary to identify the source. Usually the author's last name and the page number suffice (for example, Adams 176). If, however, you have more than one title by that author (or a title by another author with the same last name), add a short title (for example, Adams, *Emancipation* 46).

CAUTION: The *MLA* does not allow the use of *ibid.*, which is the abbreviation for the Latin *ibidem*, "in the same place." In fact, the Modern Language Association of America seems to have a phobia about ancient languages, so that it no longer allows even roman numerals for citing volume numbers. (*Chicago* is more flexible on this.) Never use *op. cit* and *loc. cit*, which are abbreviations for the Latin words meaning, respectively, "in the work cited" and "in the place cited."

☞ *Consolidation of references.* Although you must document all information, it really is overkill to have four or five note numbers in the same paragraph, all referring to the same source. Even if several different sources are used, they can often be consolidated into one note per paragraph. This practice is best illustrated in recent issues of such scholarly journals as *American Historical Review, Journal of American History,* and the *William and Mary Quarterly,* and in recent books published by American university presses.

Is one rough draft enough?

You will probably need to write at least a second rough draft, and some parts of your paper may require even more rewriting. Remember, though, that you can use your scissors and tape to incorporate anything from the first draft that needs little change. Use your dictionary to check every word about whose spelling or meaning you have any question. Use adjectives and adverbs sparingly. Make every word count. Read your paper aloud—to someone else if possible, to yourself if need be.

When you are satisfied with the content, work on clarity and elegance of expression. In writing, style does not mean florid prose. Good writing is straightforward, so that the reader does not have to ponder the meaning. Professors are impressed by well-crafted prose and likely to give an edge to its practitioners; so are recruiters and bosses in the "real world."

Becoming a good writer takes effort, but the following works will ease your way: William Zinsser, *On Writing Well;* William Strunk and E. B. White, *The Elements of Style;*[5] and Samuel Eliot Morison's essay, "History as a Literary Art."[6] Finally, if you still wonder why history should read well, instead of being merely accurate, read George Orwell's essay "Politics and the English Language."[7]

What is an annotated bibliography? A bibliographical essay? Why can't I just list my sources?

The bibliography is the last part of a formal paper. A few instructors omit the bibliography for short papers, since the necessary publication information should already be in the first citation of each source. Others require only a simple list of the works cited in the paper. More and more instructors, however, ask for a bibliography that shows how you went about researching your paper and discusses the uses and shortcomings of all the works that you consulted, not just the ones that made it into your endnotes. This may take the form of an annotated bibliography or of a bibliographical essay.

The annotated version is in formal bibliographic form, such as that in *MLA*, section 4, but with comments added (annotated) at the end of each entry. Here is an example of an annotated bibliography at the end of the chapter on the Progressive Era in Paul Boyer et al., *The Enduring Vision: A History of the American People*, 2d ed. (Lexington: D. C. Heath, 1993) chapter 22:

> Link, Arthur S., and Richard L. McCormick. *Progressivism.* Arlington Heights: Harlan Davidson, 1983. Lucid, sensible unraveling of progressivism's diverse strands and comprehensive discussion of current interpretations.
> Wiebe, Robert. *The Search for Order, 1877–1920.* New York: Hill and Wang, 1967. A highly influential study treating progressivism as a response of a new middle class and professional groups to late-nineteenth-century urban-industrial changes.

Bernard Bailyn et al., *The Great Republic*, 4th ed., vol. 2 (Lexington: D. C. Heath, 1992), uses the bibliographical essay, as in this example from chapter 6, "The Enlightenment's New World":

> The eighteenth-century colonial wars were the subject of Francis Parkman's most dramatic narratives — still immensely readable — in his nine-volume series, *France and England in North America.* His *Half-Century of Conflict* (2 vols., 1892) covers King George's War, and his *Montcalm and Wolfe* (2 vols., 1884) the French and Indian War. A modern, technical, scholarly work covering the same ground in greater detail but lacking Parkman's narrative style is Lawrence H. Gipson's *British Empire Before the American Revolution*, vols. VI–VIII (1946–53). Howard H. Peckham, *The Colonial Wars, 1689–1762* (1964), provides a brief introduction to the main events. On the British army

in pre-Revolutionary America, see John Shy, *Toward Lexington* (1965), chs. 1–3.

Note that each approach provides a kind of mini–book review. This feature makes each far more useful than a simple listing of other books on the subject covered by the chapter.

Whether you choose an annotated bibliography or a bibliographical essay, organize it in a logical way. You could, for instance, group reference works, primary (documentary) sources, books, journal articles, and so on, rather than simply listing everything in alphabetical order. The bibliography will take time, so don't leave it until the last minute. If you have written comments about each source on the back of its bib card, it will help a lot.

How do I turn my rough draft into a final copy to hand in?

The following may seem — and probably is — dogmatic, but it is worth learning a standard format for your writing. (If your instructor tells you to follow a different format from the one proposed here, you should of course use that one.)

When you are finally satisfied with your paper in rough draft, prepare the final paper. Approach the task as if you would someday send it to an editor in hopes of being paid for it, or to a boss who has the power to promote you. If you follow the conventions of a standard style manual such as *Chicago* or *MLA*, you will be able to produce copy that editors will recognize as accepted professional style, thus ensuring that your submissions get a serious, honest reading. Even if your instructor professes not to care about format and appearance, the student with a paper prepared to editorial standards usually has a decided edge.

☞ *Preparation.* Have an adequate supply of acceptable paper: white, twenty-weight, uncoated. If you are typing, duplicator bond is a good, economical choice. Rag-bond "thesis" paper, especially the stuff with red double-margin lines on all sides, is not necessary. If the watermark says something like "erasable" or "corrasible," don't use the paper. Instructors and editors hate it because it smears and won't take ink well. (If you have an electronic typewriter that requires waxed paper, hand in a photocopy.) Clean the typeface of your typewriter. Test the ribbon (this also applies to computer printers). If it is beginning to get faint, replace it. Handwritten papers (if your instructor accepts them) should be on good-quality, lined, three-ring-binder paper and must be legibly written in blue or black ink. Have some correction fluid or tape on hand. Do not erase.

☞ *Margins.* Set your margins at one-and-one-half inches on the left, one inch on the other three sides. If you are handwriting, you may rule these margins with a straightedge, in pencil. If you are using a word processor or an electronic typewriter, set ragged right, not justified right, margin.

☞ *Spacing.* Set (and leave) your typewriter or word processor on double-space. Nothing in the whole paper, including quotes and endnotes, may be anything less than double-spaced. If your instructor allows handwritten papers, write (unless your writing is really tiny) on alternating lines throughout.

☞ *The first page.* Follow the example in your style manual. Do not use a cover sheet or title page unless your instructor requests it. On the left, one inch from the top, put your name, the course, and the date, each on its own line. Double-space. Type the title, centered. Quadruple-space. Indent five spaces. Begin your first paragraph. Make sure that you hit the space bar once after internal punctuation, twice after terminal punctuation. Continue to the end of the paper, leaving one-inch margins at the top and bottom of each page.

☞ *Numbering.* Number each page about one-half inch from the top right, consecutively throughout the paper, including endnotes and bibliography.

☞ *Quotations.* Quoted matter of more than four lines should be indented ten spaces from the left and not enclosed in quotation marks. You should continue in double-space, even if your style sheet (*Chicago*) says to single-space.

☞ *Endnotes.* After you have finished the text of your paper, begin a new page. Entitle it "Endnotes." Your instructor may ask you to indicate as well which style manual (*Chicago* or *MLA*) you are using for your citations. Double-space. Type or write your endnotes double-spaced throughout. Since you have good bib cards, you will be able to do this without first making a rough draft.

☞ *Bibliography.* After the endnotes, on a new page, begin your bibliographical essay or annotated bibliography.

☞ *Corrections.* Proofreading is very important. Read over the final copy several times. At least once, read it aloud, including punctuation. Get someone else to read it if you possibly can. Double-check all the direct quotes, using the original instead of your notes if you can. Instructors (and most editors) permit brief corrections in ink, with insertions typed or written above the line. Nothing is more irritating to a reader than a paper filled with typographical errors and showing no evidence of proofreading.

CAUTION: If you have a spelling checker program for your electronic typewriter or word processor, by all means use it; but that will not spare you the task of proofreading. Spelling checkers don't catch the wrong word or the senseless sentence.

☞ *Handing it in.* Read over both the paper and the instructions one last time. Find out how the instructor wants the paper handed in. Unless specifically instructed, do not staple the pages together, because it is easier to check citations without having to flip pages back and forth. Use paper clips if you like, but they are not mandatory. Many instructors prefer that you turn in your paper in an ordinary 9" × 12" envelope with your name on it, rather than in an expensive binder. Do not seal the envelope unless you are mailing it.

Why should I keep the paper when I get it back?

When you get the paper back, go over it carefully. Read all the comments. Look up all the words that have been marked for spelling or meaning. Check all the facts that have been questioned. Keep the paper in a safe place, in an envelope with your name on it. You may need to resubmit it with the next assignment, or you may have to provide a writing sample someday, in applying for graduate school or a job. You may even be able to revise and expand the paper (after consulting the instructor) for another course. More than a few undergraduate history papers have evolved into published books and articles.

A final word: do not be dismayed by extensive comments on your paper. Sometimes the best papers warrant the most red ink, while the really bad ones are hardly worth the effort. Those comments, whether on content, grammar, or style, are part of your education. Take them to heart.

Endnotes

[1] The first edition of this book was composed on an early Macintosh with 800K floppies and no hard drive, although both my campus and my publisher were using MS-DOS. It caused only a few problems, but my present computer's hard drive, several megabytes of memory, and system translatability has made life easier.

[2] Anything that can go wrong will go wrong. *Webster's Ninth New Collegiate Dictionary* (1985 ed.).

[3] For example, see William Zinsser, *On Writing Well,* 3rd ed. (New York: Harper, 1985) 10–11.

[4] R. J. Lambrose, review of Glatt Plagiarism Services, *Lingua Franca,* February/March 1992, 6.

[5] 3rd ed. (New York: Macmillan, 1979).

[6] Originally done in 1946 as a leaflet for the Old South Association of Boston, it is reprinted in Samuel Eliot Morison, *By Land and by Sea* (New York: Knopf, 1953) 289–98, and, in a slightly shorter form, in *Harvard Guide to American History* 3–8.

[7] Originally published in 1946, it is available in most collections of Orwell's essays.

Epilogue

When your first history course has ended, what do you have? I hope that it is more than just a grade and certification that you have jumped through one of the academic hoops. If you rid yourself of everything to do with the course as soon as the final exam is over, then you've wasted time and money. Here are some things you ought to consider hanging on to:

☞ *The textbooks.* There is a great temptation to convert them into cash, but are you sure that you will never have any more questions about American history? You can look things up in the library, but having your text at hand will save time. Besides, you are familiar with the format and content. The textbook will come in handy for other, more advanced courses in history and even for courses in fields such as English, sociology, and political science. And later, believe it or not, questions about the past will arise in the "real world" outside of college, and on these occasions you will be pleased if you've kept your textbook.

☞ *Lecture notes.* You can't even sell these. If you trash them, you have thrown away a substantial part of your memory. Lecture notes, like textbooks, may be useful again, in a different context.

☞ *Bib cards.* These are part of your permanent record of reading and research. You'd be surprised how often it is necessary to recall a book you read several years ago.

☞ *Research notes.* These may also be useful again, perhaps for another course or for a project beyond college.

☞ *Papers.* As noted above, you will need them if you are asked for a writing sample — as graduate programs and many employers often do.

Finally, there is knowledge — and not just the historical facts you have learned. Some of them will stick with you, but what is more important is an understanding of how you use the facts. For a while you knew how to think historically and thus acquired one of the tools for survival. You can keep this skill if you use it, but you will surely lose it if you do not.

Some of you may even wish to convert your newfound historical skills into a career. For up-to-date answers to the question How can I make a living out of history? the American Historical Association publishes two excellent pamphlets: *Careers for Students of History,* by Barbara J. Howe (1989), and *Becoming a Historian: A Survival Manual for Women and Men,* by Melanie Gustafson (1991). Your library probably has them, or you can order your own copies from the American Historical Association, Publication Sales, 400 A Street SE, Washington, DC 20003-3889.

About the Author

Neil R. Stout is Professor of History at the University of Vermont, where he has taught since 1964, after previous teaching stints at the University of Wisconsin, Madison (1958–1960), and Texas A&M (1961–1964). He received his B.A. from Harvard in 1954 and Ph.D. from Wisconsin in 1962. He has served as president of the New England Historical Association and as director of the University of Vermont's graduate programs in history, historic preservation, and cultural history/museology. In 1992 he was named Editor of *Vermont History*, the journal of the Vermont Historical Society. His previous books include *The Royal Navy in America, 1760–1775* (1973) and *The Perfect Crisis: The Beginning of the Revolutionary War* (1976).